WISDOM INSTRUCTS HER CHILDREN

The Power of the Spirit and the Word

John Randall, S.T.D.

LIVING FLAME PRESS
LOCUST VALLEY, N.Y. 11560

Third printing 1984

Cover: Robert Manning

All scripture quotations are from the *New American Bible* and the *Jerusalem Bible*

Copyright: 1981: John Randall

Nihil Obstat: Rev. Msgr. John F. Cox, Ph.D., *Censor Librorum* March 31, 1981

Imprimatur: Louis E. Gelineau, D.D., S.T.L., J.C.L., Bishop of Providence, March 31, 1981

ISBN: 0-914544-36-5

Published by: Living Flame Press/Box 74/Locust Valley, N.Y. 11560

Printed in the United States of America

Foreword

This book has grown out of a series of ten lectures originally given in the summer of 1979 at the Catholic Charismatic Bible Institute at St. Mary's University in San Antonio, Texas. The response to them, particularly the encouragement of brothers and sisters here in Providence prompted my decision to edit and reproduce the talks in print. It is my prayer that they give glory to God and help build up the Church of Jesus Christ.

I should note that this book, a product of life in the Catholic Charismatic Renewal, is addressed to people familiar with that Renewal, its blessings and problems. That being said, I believe it can be of help to all who, like Mary, seek to be filled with the Wisdom of God.
— John Randall, Ash Wednesday, 1981

Introduction

While recently attending an ordination of permanent deacons I was deeply struck by the commission that the Bishop gave these twenty or so men: "Charles, receive the gospel of Christ whose herald you now are. Believe what you read; teach what you believe; and practice what you teach."

That says a great deal. I remembered hearing it at my own ordination over twenty-five years ago, but now it came back to me with new force. The Word is the source of our wisdom. That is the first point. This does not happen automatically, however. We have to find our home in it. As Jesus said, "Make your home in My word."[1] You have to really get into the Word; you have to make your own what you read.

The second point made in the ordination is that you should teach only what you believe; because if you do not believe it, the message will not be accepted. The Bishop said, "Believe what you read." The old Latin phrase "Nemo dat quod non habet," said it well — "You can not give what you do not have." Or, as Jesus said, "Out of the mouth comes the abundance of the heart."[2] You can get across only what you are — not all the words you may say in a Sunday homily. What is communicated is only what you have assimilated — what you have eaten. The Lord told Ezekiel and the author of Revelation, "Eat the Scroll."[3] Only what you have really believed and made your own comes across. You can only communicate the Word of God that has become flesh in you. So, believe what you read, and then teach.

The final injunction was, "practice what you teach," so that people can see it in action. Like Jesus you will then be "the Word made flesh." You will be a walking Bible. As the common adage goes, "You may be the only Bible your neighbor will ever see."

Now, let me apply that instruction of the Bishop to the deacons to what I would like to discuss in this book. I want to share with you my own convictions on wisdom. Though I have had training in Sacred Scripture and taught it for many years, for the past several years I have been away from formal teaching, occupied mostly in pastoral experiences. So, I am writing not so much out of the classroom experience of teaching wisdom as from the lived experience of what the Holy Spirit has tried to communicate to our little community in Providence. If you are expecting a very technical presentation on wisdom, you may be disappointed. It is only the wisdom the Lord has given me that I wish to communicate.

There is a beautiful verse in the breviary which reads: "May the Word of Christ ever fill your hearts. Share with one another the wisdom you receive."[4] That is what I will be attempting to do in this book.

[1] John 8:31
[2] Mark 7:21
[3] Ezekiel 3:1; Revelation 10:9
[4] Versicle from Roman Breviary, Sunday of Week I, Office of Readings.

Table of Contents

CHAPTER 1

Experiencing Wisdom —
A Personal Account

John MacKenzie wrote a book on the New Testament called *The Power and the Wisdom*. That title is a beautiful summary of what the New Testament is and of what much of the Church is lacking today. Paul says: "Many hold the form of religion but deny the power of it."[1] The Church goes through many observances, but its members often have not very deeply experienced the power of Jesus. We Christians should be able to tap this most tremendous power on earth and release it to the world!

In the renewal we hope to gain that ability. We are beginning to experience more and more of the power God has made so available. And yet we know it is just a taste of what he wants to communicate to us: the power of the Holy Spirit to heal, and to renew the face of the earth.

It is the second part of MacKenzie's title, "the Wisdom," that I would especially like to discuss in this book, however. I feel that wisdom is lagging even behind power! God wants to bring a new release of it to those renewed in the Spirit. We so terribly lack wisdom! It is somewhat understandable though; we are young yet, and wisdom usually comes with white hair according to the Bible. God the Father so wants wisdom to be increased in this world! He wants to pour much more wisdom into the world than we have even dreamed of, wisdom far beyond our wildest imaginations.

By way of illustration I would like to share with you as a witness would, my experience of being led by the Spirit. He opened my eyes to some insights that, hopefully, I can share thereby providing keys to the greater wisdom He now wants to place in His Church.

After I was ordained, I was a parish priest for six very happy years, and would have been content to remain in active ministry. However, I heard the Lord calling me to work for renewal. My Bishop asked me to go away to study and teach in our college seminary. Convinced that the main leaders of the church were priests (before Vatican II) I felt that renewal had to do mostly with work in seminaries. I gladly accepted the Bishop's call and went to the University of Louvain from 1959 — 1962 to study particularly the Word of God. I received a doctorate in theology, and did my thesis in Scripture on the gospel of John, John 17:20-22, focusing particularly on the community sense of that passage. A great love for the Word had always been with me, but it especially grew during those three years in Louvain.

When I returned, I was assigned to teach Introduction to the Bible, Old Testament and New Testament, in our college seminary. I taught only a couple of years when I was asked to reduce my teaching load and become spiritual director of the seminary. Thus, I became very involved in the renewal of seminaries and later in other spiritual renewals such as the Cursillo and Search movements in our diocese. One result of these new duties was that my formal teaching of the Word was decreasing and that my involvement in ministering the Word was increasing — a half and half ministry that proved very Providential.

The next significant happening I would like to share with you is the Baptism in the Holy Spirit experience which happened to me in 1968. The first tangible thing that I experienced occurred while celebrating Mass. I had been prayed over the night before at Teen Challenge, Dave Wilkerson's place in Brooklyn, by his brother Donald. The next morning, after very little sleep and while celebrating the 8 o'clock Mass in one of our local parish churches, it was as if I was lifted right off my feet and had an ecstatic experience of the heavens. You know the experience when the Spirit takes hold of you. I sensed the power of the Spirit in a new way at that Mass. When I should have been groggy and "out of it," everything was "ringing and singing." I had not had time to prepare the homily; but nevertheless will always remember the rare and rewarding experience I had of a man coming into the sacristy afterwards and telling me, "Father, you really hit me right between the eyes." There was no direct proportion between my effort and the flowing of the Spirit!

I would probably have lost that experience in the hustle and bustle of activities were it not for the fact that God constantly pursued me like "the hound of heaven." I was lucky to have another contact with the Baptism in the Holy Spirit some six months later. At that time we had a Cursillo leaders' workshop in Rhode Island. Paul DeCelles, from South Bend, Indiana attended and was one of the men on the workshop team. At the end of the workshop Paul bore witness, before a group of us, to the charismatic renewal at Notre Dame. It was 4 a.m. when, after listening to him throughout the night, we priests knelt down on my floor in the seminary and asked Paul, this Physics professor from Notre Dame, this scientist, to pray over us for a new inflow of the Holy Spirit. See how upside down the Spirit is making our world today! After the age of science and atheism, a scientist praying over priests! It was the first time I had ever heard a Catholic pray in tongues.

The experience that happened to me occurred several hours later. Nothing "on the spot," but around noontime of that day, after teaching classes all that morning, I picked up my breviary to pray some psalms. As I did so, the Spirit was waiting. He made the words of those psalms skip and jump and hop and leap. They just flew right out of the page at me. I am sure many of you have experienced that feeling, when a touch of the Spirit comes upon the Word. I could not get beyond one psalm. I just sat there in my chair and wept; I wept at how beautiful the Word was. I was struck and humbled. Even though I had taught the scriptures for years and had much professional training, I received more light on the Word in one flash than I had in years of study and teaching! It was as if a light, a bright light, had illuminated the Word; and I was stirred as if by a fire inside while Jesus, the living Word, emerged from that written word! The living quality of God just came alive in a way I had never dreamed possible.

About that same time I was leading a weekend workshop team for young high school people who were going to be leaders that year in the Search for Christian Maturity Program. We were trying to focus the attention of the youth on an experience of community so that they could, in turn, try to help create community around the diocese in the various Searches that would be held. The team and I worked laboriously all night Friday and all day Saturday with these young people, with considerable success. However, when the team met late Saturday night in the chapel, we were a bit dejected. Although we were approaching community from every possible angle, not much was catching fire; we knew that something was missing. We had trust exercises, psychological experiences, one-on-one talks, group discussions, group therapy; we taught from Scripture, as best we could, the concept of community. We participated in many activities together. But somehow it seemed that the kind of community that God wanted to convey was not taking root. And so, as they say, when all else fails, pray! There we were with the Master who said, "Call no one teacher but me,"[2] in the quiet chapel near midnight that Saturday night. I will never forget those moments; we just came before Him humbly, empty, and we asked Him, "Lord, What will we do? How do you get across community to these young people?" We just knelt there quietly for a while. Then I was inspired, I am sure by the Spirit, to take out my pocket New Testament. I heard the Spirit say to my spirit, "If you just take this little book, and you start to live it, you will have community." I shared the insight with the group. The Spirit was communicating the same message to everyone. They said, "Yes, Yes, Let's do that. That's it! That's the answer! We will find community as people perceive and practice the Word." I thought quickly in those moments in that chapel of how Francis did that, Francis of Assisi and Ignatius of Loyola, and other great men in renewal — simply by accepting the Word and living it.

Now, I could theologically interpret the Word with the best of them. I could demythologize, get into form and tradition criticism and all those things. But this idea of actually living that Word and learning from the experience of it was new, as new as my experiences with the Mass and the Psalms had been.

After reflecting further upon our living of the Word, an image came to mind: Flashing across a screen in front of me were the words, "The Full Gospel Businessman's Fellowship International." I began to understand the strength these men had (with all their limitations) because they were getting at the full gospel. The fullness of the Word was bringing them power they had never dreamed of, and I said, "That is it!"

The next morning we told the thirty-five young people that we were going to try an experiment. We told them we were going to give each of them a copy of the New Testament. We made a very beautiful liturgical presentation similar to that of the early catechumenate, presenting the Word very solemnly as a gift. We told them they were going to be sent out for two or three hours, the rest of the morning, and that they were going to be asked to stay in absolute silence and alone. They were to be apart, in the chapel, in their rooms, out in the fields, with nothing but the Word and the Holy Spirit. We enjoined them to pray to the Holy Spirit, conducted a brief prayer service before they left, and then we sent them out with the Word and said, "Just let the Word speak to you." Their initial response was, "How are we going to do that for so long?" We asked them to try it, and out they went. When the time had passed, we had some difficulty assembling them. It was an unforgettable, amazing experience! I honestly believe that during those three hours many young people were baptized in the Holy Spirit. Some became lay apostles that very day.

All afternoon they shared the Word and its message. One young man remarked, "Man, this book is like a map. It is like a map of life. Everything is in there." They were all equally excited. They thanked us so much for the Word and expressed their desire to study it together. From that day on, communicating the Word has become a vital part of every Search in Rhode Island. That single day's experience has had a tremendous influence. The idea of community was suddenly and effectively transferred to these youths, not as an entity itself, but as a sort of by-product that occurs when the Word of God is lived.

Community then began to form amongst us in

Rhode Island. I will not go into the details of what eventually became a large budding prayer group of 500, as we moved to Saint Patrick's Parish in Providence, but will simply say that the Lord led us to call ourselves the Word of God community.

In Ann Arbor, a kind of parent community, the Holy Spirit had already directed the community there to call their community the Word of God. We saw many advantages in doing this. The "Word of God" community began to replace words such as Pentecostal or charismatic. Everybody could accept the Word; we are all founded on the Word. We used to say at Mass, "Taught by Our Saviour's commands and formed by the Word of God, we dare to say, Our Father . . . "[3]. So, we called ourselves less and less Pentecostal or charismatic; more and more the Word of God people, the Word of God community. It is amazing what doors the Word can open.

At nearly the same time another discovery touched me as I walked with the Spirit, the discovery of two different uses of the Word in the Greek scriptures. One is "Logos" and the other is anglicized "Rayma." The "Logos," if you will, is the whole body of the Word; the Bible is the "Logos." Scripture ordinarily calls the Word "Logos." But there is another use of the Word, called "Rayma." "Rayma" is a word which means "the Word for you," the personalized Word, the "now" Word. For example, when you get a passage that speaks to you today and is given to you by the Holy Spirit, that is the "Rayma," the "Logos" that has become "Rayma." The Spirit began to teach me, scripture scholar that I was, about the "Rayma," and He would give me, day after day, the "Rayma" to lead and guide me charismatically in wondrous ways.

I was slow to yield to the full power of the baptism in the Spirit. I guess we all are. In fact, none of us have yet. As Steve Clark says, "You do not get baptized in the Spirit; you get brought into the ever-baptizing Spirit." That is what happens. You know there are stages and stages. When you think you have received it all, you have not received much yet. In a sense, the beginning of wisdom is to know how "dumb" you are. The opposite of wisdom is pride, to think that you have it all. Well, I was not praying in tongues yet. And with my scriptural expertise I was teaching that tongues was not for everybody! Paul lists different kinds of gifts: Some speak in tongues, some have interpretation, some prophesy, some have administration, and so forth. I had not spoken in tongues; I was baptized in the Spirit. Therefore, tongues was not for everybody! Person after person argued with me about this idea. They asked me if I would be willing to be prayed over; still nothing happened. All kinds of national leaders prayed over me to no avail. Then one day, Judy Tydings from the Mother of God community in Potomac, Maryland, was in Providence and she gave a teaching at our prayer meeting. Afterward she said, "Jake, have you ever prayed in tongues?"

I said, "What! Another one!"

She said, "I really believe the Lord wants you to pray in tongues."

I said, "Well, I am open to it, I thought."

She told me to kneel down and try to imitate the

sounds that she was making, a way of priming the pump. "Then, if the Spirit puts a word or two into your mind," she said, "let it flow forth." I obediently began to pray, and a couple of crazy sounds went through my mind; I began to stammer them. She said, "That is it."

I said, "What!" You see, I had seen people begin to speak in tongues with a tremendous flow, with no doubt about it. This, however, was not my experience.

Then she said, "Now go home and practice that; keep doing it. Like a baby learning to say 'da, da, da,' you have got to learn to grow in a new language." I thought, this is crazy, and I had no intention of doing it.

After the meeting that night, I shared my irritation with two leaders of our prayer group, but got absolutely no sympathy from them. "Thank God!" They said, "she is right. You need to yield to tongues. There is so much more for you, Jake, if you can."

I replied, "We are doing all right now." We argued for about an hour, sitting in the car outside where we were living, and finally one of them said, "Well, look, you believe in the Holy Spirit. You believe in getting the 'Rayma.' I think that we should pray and that you should ask the Lord to give you a 'Rayma' about your praying in tongues." They prayed in tongues and I was praying quietly. Then I opened the Scriptures to John. This "Rayma" turned me right around, as many "Raymas" have. The passage my eyes fell on was about Nicodemus, and the words were, "and you are a doctor in Israel and you do not know these things." It went on to say, "We speak of what we know, but you do not receive our testimony. Flesh begets flesh and Spirit begets Spirit."[4] I was convicted, and said, "Okay, I will yield." At that moment in the car I began to yield to these crazy sounds. I just began to babble them. I had released my mind, given up control of my intellectual faculties. I had created a vacuum through which the Spirit could flow, even as I babbled new and crazy sounds.

As I turned off, the image came to me of turning off conversing, and turning on the radio. A new sound comes in as you turn off, much like a transistor radio when you turn it on. I turned myself off fully for the first time perhaps in my life, and began to babble like a baby, being willing to be born again of a whole new life. As I turned off and babbled, my mind was freed. The Spirit flowed through the vacuum that was created. All kinds of words began to emerge. There was a flow of words of wisdom going right through my mind as I was babbling in this strange language. I remember them still. The words were in rapid succession: "Unless you become like little children, you will not enter the kingdom of heaven";[5] and the words of Paul, "If anyone thinks he is wise, he had better become a fool";[6] and the third word was from John, the book of Revelation, "I was in the Spirit one day and praying."[7] All of these words made absolute sense to me then. I knew what they meant. I had touched base, through experience, with the early church. The Spirit brought me right back there. All fears of what the Bishop would say when I spoke in tongues were gone. I was experiencing a whole new world that opened up, whole new rivers of the Spirit, rivers of wisdom flowing into me through this encounter. It is a world that has not ceased.

The next experience that developed for me and for our community was that the Lord began to lead us to give workshops. We gave a couple of workshops at the Notre Dame Conferences entitled, "Formed by the Word of God." The basis of the workshops were these two phrases: the one "Formed by the Word of God we say, Father," from the liturgy, and secondly, Romans 8:14, "Those who are led by the Spirit of God are the sons of God." We tried to give a workshop that would help people gain the same experience that God was giving us; namely, to be formed by the Word, the "Logos" and the "Rayma." It is the Spirit who gives the "Rayma," the Spirit leading us individually and as a community.

The Spirit was leading our community, in a particular way, through the "Rayma."

Let me give you an instance. During our first summer together as a community we worked in the inner city with great success. For our second summer, we figured we would do the same thing. But when we began to pray, the Lord closed all doors. We could not get the apartments we had the previous summer. Our efforts were to no avail. Then someone out in the country offered us the use of a farm. It was across the bay, out in the country, an hour or so away from the city, where our apostolate was. We said, "No, No." But nothing opened in the city. We had no place to go. Finally we said, "Let us pray." Again, when all else fails! The extent to which you lack the Spirit, even in the renewal is amazing. As a small group of us prayed that night, I opened the Scriptures for a "Rayma." My eyes fell on the beginning of John 6. It said, "And he led them across the waters to a quiet place." He put the same kind of word in the rest of the group. So we went across the waters to that farm — foolishness to us in terms of evangelization, but the Lord had His plans! He wanted to take us out and form us. He wanted to mold us into a tightly knit community. We went there and He provided for us. We had no money, no resources; yet He provided marvelously for us. He drew people there on weekends. He drew people from all over to that farm. We began to give retreats; and what we were learning, we were passing on to other prayer groups.

That house became a center of learning the Word more deeply and of growing in wisdom. While we were there, He said, "Just obey Me and I will take care of the community in Providence. Do not worry. If you obey Me, I will take care of it." While we were down there in the country, just coming up to the city once a week for the prayer meeting, the community doubled! We learned that obedience to the Word, when you are led by the Spirit and formed by His Word, "Logos" and "Rayma," makes great things possible.

The next door to wisdom that through experience, opened before me, was this. It happened in the 1974 Notre Dame Conference, the famous meeting where healing became a major factor in the renewal. I was part of the Word Gift Unit on the stage and the Lord kept pursuing me, guiding me; He wanted me to open up to prophecy. I had not prophesied in four or five years of renewal. It was not for me, I thought! Scripture scholar that I was, "dumb" Scripture scholar that I was! Paul says, "I want you all to prophesy."[8] The Spirit began to gnaw at me. "Jake, I want you to prophesy. I want you to open to prophecy," and He began to nudge me with the constant "Rayma" I would receive from I Corinthians 14, "I want you all to prophesy." I finally said, I have got to learn how to yield to prophecy; through some teaching, and with the help of friends, I did. As in past experiences, I could feel the Spirit within me now for I was no longer limiting Him to the "Rayma" or the "Logos." Just through prophecy the Spirit could come to me, speak to me, use me, use me in ways that He wanted to. So whole new avenues opened there that have been flowing ever since.

The last thing I want to share is the radio program that He led us into in late 1976. Particularly moved by Pope Paul VI's *Evangelii Nuntiandi* letter on evangelism, we felt inspired to step out in faith, secure fifteen minutes of radio time and trust God for the money to pay for it. In a largely Catholic state there was no daily Catholic radio program at that time. There was much evangelism but not a single Catholic program. We did not have any funds or resources, but the Spirit said, "Step out and I will take care of it." We did. In late 1976, we began with a program teaching the Word. We asked the Lord for a title for the program. In prayer He gave us "The Spirit and The Word." That is a very interesting combination for wisdom. The path to wisdom is the Spirit *and* the

Word. Not just the Word alone or the Spirit alone. I think, incidentally, that is where much of the weakness of the Evangelicals and some Pentecostals comes from. Evangelicals become so wrapped up in the Word that it becomes law. On the other hand, some Pentecostals are moved just by the Spirit and the result is "illuminism." But when you put the Spirit and the Word together, wow! You have power, order; the renewal of the face of the earth! When the Spirit touches the Word, it comes alive and wisdom begins to flow.

I remember a whole debacle that took place once in our Church, and I was very involved in it. It was called in Catechetics a salvation history trend. The way to reach the people of America, particularly the young people, we thought, was through salvation history — teaching them the Bible. We geared our-selves up in Rhode Island; I taught courses to teachers, and we went into salvation history for about a year. Then it flopped, fizzled. Kids were not in-terested at all in Esau, Jacob and the like. Why did it fail? Because it was the Word alone without the Spirit! Those were pre-charismatic days, the Word without the Spirit.

Our radio program, "The Spirit and the Word," was blessed by the Lord; it began to support itself although many said it would not. After six months of the program, the Spirit said, "I want you to get My Word out more." So we stepped out in faith and added another fifteen minutes. We had a half hour daily of teaching the Word and what the Spirit was saying. What we tried to teach was not just book after book, not just "Logos" but also the "Rayma." We had formed a ministry of prayer called the Bethany Ministry of Prayer and Evangelization; we would pray, asking the Lord what Word He wanted to communicate to His people that week, and teach the Word He inspired us to select. It is amazing how successful we were! The small audience grew and grew. What happened was that people were clamoring for the Word, for what the Spirit was saying. I would estimate there are 5,000 listeners to this program everyday.

Later, we expanded to one hour our teaching the Word of God through the Spirit to the people of Rhode Island and Southeastern Massachusetts. The format is in two parts. During the first half hour, the "Rayma," or "now" teaching, as we hear it, is addressed to the church of that area. Throughout the second half hour we try to make available the wisdom that God has been storing up for more than ten years in our renewal. There is a tremendous store of wisdom here. All kinds of tapes, for example, are now available to us. I remember Ralph Martin saying once at Steubenville that nobody in the whole world had any excuse today for not having wisdom, for not knowing what God is saying to the church. He said, "I do not care, you could be an Eskimo in an igloo at the North Pole and still not have any excuse. All you would need is a tape recorder with some good batteries and some tapes. Because it is all there." The wisdom is there; ten years ago it was not there. When the Catholic Charismatic renewal began, we had to draw on all types of sources, some of which were questionable. But today the wisdom that God has stored up in His church through the renewal is definitely there and we are trying to make it more available to His people. That is our aim in the second half hour, to constantly expose people to different kinds of wisdom teaching that have come forth.

What I learned and what I wanted to share with you by relating some of my personal experiences is that wisdom is a gift given by God. There is no comparison between the effort expended in seeking wisdom and the results. Wisdom is the Holy Spirit touching us. With so little effort, enormous results are realized. After years and years of hard Biblical study with seemingly minimal benefits, seeing young men leave the seminary as I taught them and so on, now, with nothing except maybe a "Rayma," hundreds of people are touched. Wisdom is truly a gift. The end of Sirach 51 says this, "I labored little, but found much." I used to labor a lot and get discouraged, but now with the gift of wisdom there is no comparison between the effort I put in and the result that appears.

The second thing I learned is that the vistas of wisdom are ever widening. That is why I shared with you every experience, every new entry into the ever-baptizing Spirit. Each time I opened up more to this flowing Spirit, new and widening vistas of wisdom began to appear. It was like watching the sky open up, and even with the mind-blowing perspectives of my experience, I know I have not begun to tap the beginning of it all yet. "How infinite His vast domain," and like a little child, I want more and more of it.

The third point I make is that this wisdom is available to us! I am going to try to share with you the keys to this wisdom that I have discovered. What God is saying, what the Spirit is saying is, "Look, my children, I want to make all my wisdom available to you, to all of you. It is there for the seeking and the asking. Wisdom you never dreamed of is available. 'Come to the waters and drink. You do not need any money; it is without price.' All you have to be is poor, broken, weak and hungry. Come if you are little." The Book of Sirach says, "Come you untutored and take up lodging in the house of instruction . . . "[9] "Father, I give you thanks," Jesus said, "that you have hidden this wisdom from the wise and the clever," (even theologians and the university professors) "and revealed it to little ones,"[10] to mere babies. We look upon Mary, although she was an uneducated young girl, as the Seat of Wisdom, don't we?

Sometimes in the renewal we hear criticism such as: "Who do you think you are?" "You got the mind of Christ or something?" "What, have you got a pipeline to God?" If anybody ever says that, you have a marvelous opportunity to evangelize. Do not miss it. Let me quote, I Corinthians 2, where Paul says, "Of the wisdom we have received, it is written: Eye has not seen, ear has not heard, nor has it so much as dawned on man what God has prepared for those who love him. Yet God has revealed this wisdom to us through the Spirit." Note that "has revealed" is a past tense, not a present tense verb; therefore, God *has* made it available! I used to think that that was a passage for heaven. What eye has not seen, someday we will see. What ear has not heard, someday we will hear. That is not what Paul says. "What eye has not seen, what ear has not heard, what no mind has imagined, God *has made available* to us through the Spirit!" What I am saying is that there is a treasure out there, brothers and sisters. "The Spirit scrutinizes all matters, even the deep things of God." "Who, for example, knows a man's innermost self but the man's own spirit within him?"[11] For instance, who knows what you are thinking right now except yourself, your spirit?

> "Similarly, no one knows what lies at the depth of God but the Spirit of God. The Spirit we have received is not the world's spirit but God's Spirit, helping us to recognize the gifts he has given us. We speak of these, not in words of human wisdom, but in words taught by the Spirit, thus interpreting spiritual things in spiritual terms. The natural man, (our critic), does not accept what is taught by the Spirit of God. For him, that is absurdity. He can not come to know such teaching because it must be appraised in a spiritual way. The spiritual man, on the other hand, can appraise everything, although he himself can be appraised by no one. For 'Who has known the mind of the Lord so as to instruct him? But we have the mind of Christ!' "[12]

My brothers and sisters, in response to the criticism often offered, "Who do you think you are? You got the mind of Christ or something?", the Church must answer with Paul, "Yes, we do have the mind of Christ!" The body of Christ, without the mind of Christ, after all, would be a freak, would it not?

1 2 Timothy 3:5
2 Matthew 23:10
3 Formula from the former Roman ritual introducing the Our Father
4 John 3:6
5 Matthew 18:3
6 I Corinthians 3:18
7 Revelation 1:10
8 I Corinthians 14:1, 3, 9
9 Sirach 51:23
10 Matthew 11:25
11 I Corinthians 2:11
12 I Corinthians 2:11-16

CHAPTER 2

Wisdom and Suffering

The Christian is not exempt from suffering; the disciple is not above his master. Jesus never promised us that we would not suffer, but He did say we would never be in confusion. Suffering yes, but confusion never. He does not want it! If you are in confusion, therefore, He wants to lead you out of it and He will show you a way.

Let us take a particular word now from the Wisdom literature, from Sirach, Chapter 4. This was originally written in Hebrew, but it was lost until very recently discovered in one of the Qumran caves. Therefore, it was commonly known only in Greek and for that reason was never put into the Hebrew canon and is missing in some Bibles. But it is the real Word of God.

I am going to start with verse 11 of Chapter 4. "Wisdom instructs her children and admonishes those who seek her. He who loves her loves life." Incidentally, wisdom is being personified here as a "She" because the Hebrew word was feminine, and so the pronoun for it was feminine. This idea led eventually to a whole wide theology of wisdom personified as a woman. In fact, many concepts reflect this mode of expression. Lady Wisdom speaks and then Dame Folly responds. After its appearance in the Wisdom literature, the Holy Spirit and Christian tradition take this personification of wisdom and develop it further into an attribute of God. In still later tradition it is also attributed in a special way to Mary as "Seat of Wisdom." In any case, wisdom here in the first instance refers to the Holy Spirit. So, "Wisdom instructs her children." You might say God instructs His children. Wisdom instructs her children "and admonishes those who seek her." If you need a little slap on the wrist, He will give it to you because He loves you. A little "tough love" that is from God. However, in addition to the admonishment at the outset, ultimately "those who seek her out, win her favor. He who holds her fast inherits glory." You have got to hang on to her hand. As Mommy says to little Joey. "Hang on to Mommy's hand." Do not let go as you go through the dark. "He who holds her fast inherits glory; wherever he dwells, the Lord bestows blessings. Those who serve her serve the Holy One; those who love her, the Lord loves. He who obeys her judges nations; he who hearkens to her dwells in her inmost chamber." He is taken right into intimate love with God. "If one trusts her, he will possess her; his descendents too will inherit her."

Now, here is the rub, the next two verses. I think it might cast light on some of your spiritual experiences. At least I have found them to be very helpful. You can not imagine God doing this kind of thing unless you read Job and this passage. But here is what God says He does in the normal walk of every Christian who is growing up. This happens after one's baptism in the Spirit experience and the honeymoon experience of being on "cloud nine" with the Lord. Wisdom then "walks with him as a stranger, and at first she puts him to the test; fear and dread she brings upon him and tries him with her discipline." Seems kind of cruel, does it not? It is an example of the tough love I was just talking about. It is similar to the excellent football coach who puts his players through their paces in training camp because he wants them to win the Super Bowl. He loves them; he does not let them slack off in their jogging, their exercising and so forth. He tests them; he tries them. He makes them tough; he teaches them the fundamentals. Thus, you have to understand what God does some time after the honeymoon is over and the trials come upon us. We say, "Where are you Lord? What is happening?" He tells us in his Word where He is and what He is doing if we listen to Him carefully. We must listen, however, to all that God says in His Word.

What we are talking about here is normal Christian experience. It is reflected in all the mystical writings, like John of the Cross' *Dark Night of the Soul* or St. Teresa's *Interior Castles*. It is reflected in all desert experiences that Christians normally go through. Scripture tells us about them; it warns us about them. Do not say "God has left me! God has abandoned me!" What He is doing is told in Sirach 4:17, which you have approached in your Christian walk; that is all it means.

In Sirach 4:17, wisdom puts them to the test, "Fear

and dread she brings upon him." We are no better than Jesus who sweated blood in Gethsemani. "And she tries him with her discipline; with her precepts she puts him to the proof." Look at this next beautiful line, it tells the answer. "She puts him to the proof until his heart is fully with her." You might underline that in your Bible. What does God want from us? He wants hearts that are fully with him! He does not want sunshine Christians. He wants day time and night time Christians, beautiful weather and stormy weather Christians. He wants desert Christians and oasis Christians who will stick with him through thick and thin, through hell and high water. He wants people going right up to the Cross, getting on it and letting him change the world by having them die and be raised with him. There is no other way. That is the pattern. There is no other pattern for the Christian, for the Christian individually, or the Christian Church. We must conform to the pattern of Jesus crucified and risen. That is ultimate wisdom, to be conformed to Jesus crucified and risen.

God never abandons us. He is always present to guide and direct our course. It is a little like you are an airplane pilot and the clouds have come and now you are navagating on radar, not by sight. You would not know where you were except by your instruments. It is the same way for the Christian. God, through faith and the Holy Spirit, will always tell you where you are. You are flying by instruments, not by sight; you are living by faith. You will not see the ground from the air but in faith, through the Spirit, in prayer, God will say, "It is all right, you are just at Sirach 4:17."

So, you continue to fly in your airplane and you are not afraid. Your radar, which is your faith, is coming through. God is walking with you, seemingly as a stranger.

I remember a word of Catherine of Siena to the Lord once. "Lord, where were you when I was going through all those trials?"

He said, "I was right at your side, proud of you as you were getting tall, walking like Jesus."

"She walks with him as a stranger, and at first she puts him to the test." It is as if God is going to sort out the Palm Sunday Christians from the Good Friday Christians. Remember the big crowds on Palm Sunday. "Hosannah," they shouted, when it was easy, like at the big charismatic conferences with everybody shouting, "Praise God!" But how many were left on Good Friday? Only the "tough lovers" were left. It was through them that God changed the world. It was through the Good Friday people that He changed the world, not the Palm Sunday people. Remember what Jesus said to Peter and to the disciples, "We are going up to Jerusalem."

Peter said, "What! Do not do that!"

Jesus replied, "Get behind me, Satan. Your ways are human. You do not know the ways of God. We are going up to Jerusalem. We are going up to Calvary."

"No disciple is above his master;" every Christian goes through Calvary. Every Christian, every prayer group, every community goes up to Jerusalem. They all want to stay in the Galilean days of miracles and happy green fields and nice trips on a boat and the like.

But, Jesus said, "We are going up to Jerusalem."

He is our wisdom, that is why Paul exalts the Cross as wisdom. We see that in I Corinthians Paul said, "Greeks seek wisdom and Jews seek sign; but we preach Christ crucified. This is scandal to the Jews and folly to the Greeks," but he who is experiencing salvation identifies with the Cross and raises it high. This is what God is looking for; therefore, it is a necessary part of our walk; we have to go through that testing. We have to go through spring training; we have to go through that football camp. We have to go through boxing match preparation in camp. Otherwise you get clobbered by a Mohammed Ali when you get into the ring; God does not want his children clobbered, because we are facing a greater adversary than a Mohammed Ali, we are facing Satan. Principalities and powers are our enemies, not flesh and blood! God wants his children to be toughened up, and because He loves us, He does this for us; it is great love. If you really understand it, it is even greater love than baptism in the Spirit.

Abbot David Geraets in a beautiful little book, *The Baptism of Suffering,* shows that suffering is a much more powerful baptism than the baptism in the Holy Spirit. I really believe that. We are talking about another baptism, one in which you become a tried and tested Christian. This is spoken of in many places in Scripture. In James 1, for example, and in I Peter 1, "God tries man like fire tries gold in the furance of humiliation" until our hearts are fully with Him, until we are no longer Palm Sunday Christians, but we are Good Friday Christians, committed to Jesus no matter what. Like the martyrs in the arenas in Rome, our lives are totally consecrated to Him. He is our all. We love Him now with our whole heart and our whole soul and our whole mind. God has attracted us with His gifts; He has given us all kinds of gifts. That is the baptism in the Spirit experience. And then He says, as we would say, "I wonder if they love me for my gifts or for myself?" So, He takes the gifts away or seems to diminish them a bit, even though they never really disappear. They are just exercised now in faith. He wants to bring us to the point where we are in love with Him, where our hearts are firm — like a tried and tested marriage of a couple who are more in love twenty-five years later than on the first day of their marriage. That is the way it should be. Their marriage has been tried and tested in the furnance of various trials as the two become one. It is the same way with God; God wants a bride. He wants a faithful bride; He wants a Mary bride standing at the foot of the Cross, hanging in there, eyes only on Jesus. That is what He wants, that is why Mary is called the Seat of Wisdom. And that is how we become seats of wisdom.

All of these things God does to His children can be likened to the father who wants his son to be a good boxer, or the mother who wants her daughter to be able to make it through all the various trials in college and every place else she goes on her own. So she gets her ready, sometimes with things the daughter may not want to do, like learning household chores and cooking. She loves her daughter; she will prepare her. That is what God does until our hearts are fully with Him.

Now, let us look at the reward; listen to this next

part of Sirach, verse 18. "Then she comes back to bring him happiness and reveal her secrets to him. But if he fails her, she will abandon him and deliver him into the hands of the despoiler." Or you make another lap around the desert like the Israelites of old, forty laps for forty years. "Another lap around the desert," God says. Many of us are making our twenty-third, twenty-fourth lap right around this time. I remember Bob Mumford talking on this subject. He said, "They took a lot of laps, but they could have made that journey in something like a couple of months, instead of forty years." And he added, "Same way with us." Many of the Israelites, Mumford commented, not only took forty laps around the desert but also ended up "blessed bones" because they could not keep their eyes on the Lord and follow His guidance.

"She comes back to him to bring him happiness and reveal her secrets to him." Here is where wisdom comes in. God promises us a second level of wisdom after the testing, after the trials. When God now can trust you, He will reveal to you deeper secrets than you have ever had before. He will reveal to you constant wisdom. You will be growing through the purgative, illuminative and unitive stages of spiritual life. He can trust you now. You are a tried and trusted friend, like His Mother and John at the foot of the Cross. You are supposed to be having this kind of union with God. In it He will reveal His deeper secrets to you. You will begin to feel strengthened by a constant source of power, never before dreamed of because you now can operate by faith and not just by sensual phenomena. You are operating by faith and you succeed because faith never fails. That is the whole point of John of the Cross and Theresa of Avila's writings. You are being brought to this dimension and it is great. You do not care whether the sun is shining or not; you are on radar. Your faith is good radar equipment. You have the Holy Spirit.

Let me use another comparison: when you are being baptized in the Spirit, at first you go into a spiritual honeymoon. Not everyone comes into this honeymoon, but many do. Some go right into the faith experience and can hardly recognize that they have been baptized in the Spirit. This is beautiful. They skip a step. Do not get discouraged if you have never experienced tremendous sensations. Maybe God has brought you right into deep faith. If you are operating that way and you know what God is saying, fine.

But, to get back to the average person, baptism in the Spirit is similar to being taken out of a rowboat where one is sweating and rowing, and put into a sailboat. The sail is the Holy Spirit and He seems to wisk you along with a new power, where there is no comparison between your effort and the distance you are covering. You are in the sailboat now; the sun is shining and the sea is beautiful. It is a great day as you are joyful and full of song. What else could you do? You are happy, you love everybody. You are in that sailboat on a beautiful day with a nice breeze. That is baptism in the Holy Spirit. Then the storm comes up, and the squall hits. Would you like to be in a sailboat when a storm wind approaches, the waves get high, rain is pouring down and it is lightning and thundering? No! So, God has another boat for you. Do you know what kind of boat? It is a submarine! What does a submarine do? Because God loves us, He takes us out of that sailboat and wants to take us into that submarine. As we go down, we scream, holler, and yell. God says, "Just trust me, trust me." So He puts us in this submarine and we go down deep, deep, deep, deep. I remember when the Nautilus first made its cruise under the North Pole. It was going through the North Pole waters as if it were going through the Gulf of Mexico. It was so deep, everything was calm and peaceful. Its radar was working well. It could go anywhere. Everything was calm. There could have been hurricanes on the surface, lightning, thunder, but the Nautilus experienced undisturbed tranquility. Picture the captain down there reading his Bible going, "dum, da, da," while everyone up above is freezing. God takes people deep.

Often times the question arises, "Why read the Wisdom literature?" My first reaction to that question is to relate an experience. I was very humbled once in talking with an ascetical theologian about all the phenomena of the charismatic renewal shortly after my involvement in it. He asked me if I knew "where ascetical theologians place all these phenomena in the three stages of spiritual life: the purgative, the illuminative and the unitive stages." He said that the phenomena of the charismatic renewal were placed in the first stage, the purgative stage. They are placed there because they are like initial graces, "come-on" graces, introductory graces to take one into faith. Not that they should not continue to operate. They should continue to operate through all the stages. I will mention later my thoughts about prayer groups that sometimes become too sophisticated and let the gifts (prophecy and tongues, for example) go. Although these gifts are present in all the stages of spiritual life, they are normally placed in the first. Some of the most powerful experiences of prophecy and tongues that I have ever heard, God had given to people who seemed the farthest away from Him. I once witnessed a new convert get so "zapped" that he came out with a fifteen minute peroration in a beautiful flowing tongue. That was from someone who hardly knew the Lord, at the purgative stage. The gifts have nothing to do with sanctity. They are for the building of the body and the person.

I wanted to share this chapter with you as a kind of sequel to the wisdom books' story of Job. Who was Job? He was a good man being tested. So if you are suffering intensely, and God gives you the book of Job or a speech of Job, then say to yourself, "Well, okay, I am being tested. My Father is putting a heavier sparring partner in the ring with me today than He put yesterday." Sirach 4 explains and further develops Job in that point of testing. God tests and strengthens us, strengthens our muscles, builds up our minds, builds up our hearts, makes us tough lovers, sturdy, dependable, day in and day out lovers of God. Remember Gideon; God said to him, "You have too many troops." He may be saying that to the whole charismatic renewal. "Hey, you have too many. Get rid of your 30,000 and get it down to 10,000. Or, you still have too many, get them down to 300," 300 tried and tested men and women, 300 spiritually strong people who would know two things. First of all, they would be ready for anything, and secondly, they would know that if the victory comes, it would not be their victory but God's. That is wisdom.

* I Corinthians 1:22

CHAPTER 3

Our Wisdom Heritage

Let me briefly trace our heritage of Wisdom by taking a rapid trip through the Bible, highlighting a few of
the more outstanding passages. My purpose is to open
up some of the vistas I have mentioned previously,
tremendous vistas that we are just beginning to
discover. In the renewal we have touched upon much
power; we have yet to unveil much of the wisdom
that the New Testament opens up to us.

Suppose the sons of John D. Rockefeller or Paul
Getty were unaware of their parentage and thought
they were born in the slums with no inheritance. That
is how we Christians often are! We feel poor and we
do not know our inheritance. We are unaware of our
birth right. There is a story that used to be told in our
life in the Spirit seminars, a kind of modern parable
that bears repeating. It is the story of an immigrant
family who came to this country from Europe some
time ago, when America was the land of opportunity.
The father wanted to provide this opportunity to his
children. So, he literally sold all he had and put his
family on a boat that was going to take a ten or twelve
day trip to America. With the few sous he had left, he

bought some bread and cheese for the journey. Since the family was poor and humble, they gathered in part of the hold of the ship, way down below sea level. They stayed by themselves, fearful of the rest of the world. They did not speak the same language as many of the other people, so they stayed by themselves, waiting to arrive in America, the land of opportunity. Day after day they stayed there, eating bread and cheese, bread and cheese, and the cheese was becoming harder and the bread was becoming more stale; but they kept eating bread and cheese, bread and cheese. Finally, about half way across the ocean, the teenage son (teenagers are usually the first to rebel) rebelled. He was gone all day and the father and mother did not dare follow him. They were simply angry and in consternation. Around midnight the son came whistling back to the family, happy, a lilt in his step. He said, "Hi Dad!"

"Where were you?" His father stormed.

"Dad, I had a great day. You would not believe it," the son answered. "For lunch I had steak and they served red wine, beautiful wine with the steak, and strawberry shortcake for dessert. And tonight they had Southern fried chicken. They served white wine with that, beautiful, sweet white wine and peach melba for dessert."

And the father said, "Where did you steal the money for that?"

The son quickly replied, "Dad, I found out it came with the price of the ticket!"

That is a parable to illustrate that we do not know our heritage. We are like that family in the hold, eating bread and cheese. Ninety-eight per cent of Christians are in the hold, eating bread and cheese, when they could be having steak, strawberry short-cake and red wine.

Let us discover some of this unknown heritage. We might begin by looking at this passage from Moses' Canticle, Deuteronomy 32:12, 15, 19: "The Lord alone was their leader." When this was so, the story goes on, they grew very prosperous. They grew so prosperous that in verse 15, "Jacob ate his fill, the darling grew fat and frisky, fat and gross and gorged. They spurned the God who made them and scorned their saving Rock." God was so good to them. When He alone was their leader, they became prosperous but then they forgot, like modern America, what God had done. We too have become fat and prosperous and we have forgotten God. "In God We Trust," it says on our coins; we really do not; so He is taking all coins away and making them valueless.

The next stop in our heritage voyage is Numbers 9:15. This is the story of the cloud by day and the pillar of fire by night. Look at this passage in the context of the Lord alone wanting to lead Israel. This is the story of the tent, God's tent, being erected every day as the Israelites went through the desert.

"On the day when the Dwelling was erected, the cloud covered the Dwelling, the tent of the commandments; but from evening until morning it took on the appearance of fire over the Dwelling. It was always so: during the day the Dwelling was covered by the cloud, which at night had the appearance of fire. Whenever the cloud rose from the tent, the Israelites would break camp; wherever the cloud came to rest, they would pitch camp. At the bidding of the Lord the Israelites moved on, and at his bidding they encamped. As long as the cloud stayed over the Dwelling they remained in camp.

"Even when the cloud tarried many days over the Dwelling the Israelites obeyed the Lord and would not move on;"

They refused to get ahead of the Lord!

"yet sometimes the cloud was over the Dwelling only for a few days. It was at the bidding of the Lord that they stayed in camp, and it was at his bidding that they departed. Sometimes the cloud remained there only from evening until morning; and when it rose in the morning, they would depart. Or if the cloud lifted during the day, or even at night, they would set out. (even in the middle of the night!) Whether the cloud tarried over the Dwelling for two days or for a month or longer, the Israelites remained in camp and did not depart; but when it lifted, they moved on. Thus, it was always at the bidding of the Lord that they encamped, and at his bidding that they set out; ever heeding the charge of the Lord, as he had bidden them through Moses."

Again an illustration that for the Israelites, the Lord alone was their leader. They were just obeying Him. When the Lord said, "Go left," they went left. When the Lord said, "Go right," they went right. When the Lord said, "Stop," they stopped. When He said, "Go," they went. That kind of sensitivity to the will of the Lord is ultimate wisdom.

There are all kind of places in the books of the Pentateuch where Moses is described as going to the meeting tent. Did you ever see that expression, "the meeting tent?" What did Moses do there? He talked to God, got the marching orders for the day, and the Israelites went on. The meeting tent is the place where God met Moses and where Moses talked to God, as friend to friend. They talked and walked and listened to each other. Moses received God's word and promise and trusted in that promise. Thus, he is depicted as God's friend who had a great intimacy with him. He knew God and God led him.

Next there is an amusing and beautiful story about Elisha the prophet in 2 Kings, chapter 6, verse 8 — amusing for the Israelites, but not for the enemy. Israel was at war with Aram.

> "When the king of Aram was waging war on Israel, he would make plans with his servants to attack a particular place. But the man of God would send word to the king of Israel. 'Be careful! Do not pass by this place, for Aram will attack there.' So the king of Israel would send word to the place which the man of God had indicated, and alert it; then they would be on guard. This happened several times.
>
> "Greatly disturbed over this, the king of Aram called together his officers. 'Will you not tell me,' he asked them, 'who among us is for the king of Israel?'"

Who is the traitor in my camp giving them all my signals?

> "'No one, my lord king,' answered one of the officers. 'The Israelite prophet Elisha can tell the king of Israel the very words you speak in your bedroom.' 'Go, find out where he is,' he said, 'so that I may take him captive.'"

You see the wisdom of Israel! See how God saved Israel by wisdom through the Word.

The prophet Amos next reveals some thoughts that we should stress, thoughts that remain true today. Amos 3:7, "Indeed the Lord God does nothing without revealing his plans to his servants, the prophets." Isn't that beautiful? See why there should be no confusion in the Christian camp! "The Lord God does nothing without revealing his plans to his servants." God not only has plans, but He also sent His Son Jesus and the Holy Spirit to reveal those plans.

Isaiah 30:20 contains a promise that God made to Israel after the exile. "The Lord will give you the bread you need," after the famine.

> "The Lord will give you the bread you need and the water for which you thirst.
> "No longer will your Teacher hide himself, but with your own eyes you shall see your Teacher,
> "While from behind, a voice shall sound in your ears: 'This is the way; walk in it,' when you would turn to the right or to the left.
> "And you shall consider unclean your silver-plated idols and your gold-covered images;
> "You shall throw them away like filthy rags to which you say, "Begone!"'

That promise is not made to the prophet alone. We too are to know what the Lord is saying to us. His promise is for all the people of Israel, in the days of the Messiah, in the days of the new and coming covenant; therefore, it is made to us. "We are the sons and daughters of the prophets." We are told in the New Testament that we are their heirs.

Another promise of the new covenant, on the same

idea as Isaiah's is found in Jeremiah 31:31. This promise again makes reference to a new covenant, after the
exile, a time in which we are now living.

> The days are coming, says the Lord, when I
> will make a new covenant with the house of Israel
> and the house of Judah. It will not be like the cove-
> nant I made with their fathers the day I took them
> by the hand to lead them forth from the land of
> Egypt; for they broke my covenant and I had to
> show myself their master, says the Lord. But this
> is the covenant which I will make with the house
> of Israel after those days, says the Lord. I will
> place my law within them, and write it upon their
> hearts; I will be their God, and they shall be my
> people. No longer will they have need to teach
> their friends and kinsmen how to know the Lord.
> All, from least to greatest, shall know me, says the
> Lord, for I will forgive their evildoing and
> remember their sin no more."

Isn't that fantastic? Particularly when you know
what the Hebrew word "know" really means. The
Hebrew word "know" used here is not the Greek intellectual "know." The Hebrew word "know" is best
translated "experience." As in Genesis, Adam
"knew" Eve and she conceived. That is what the
Hebrew word "know" means. You experience God.
You have an intimate union with God. His life flows
into you. It is a total reality, not just intellectual, a
coming into union with God. What the new covenant
promises is that all God's people will experience him.
No teachers will be needed. Brother will not have to
teach brother nor kinsman his kinsman. CCD (Con-
fraternity of Christian Doctrine) teachers should put

themselves out of business once people have experienced the Lord for themselves.

The prophet of the exile, Ezekiel, comes next. Ezekiel 36:25:

"I will sprinkle clean water upon you to cleanse you from all your impurities, and from all your idols I will cleanse you. I will give you a new heart and place a new spirit within you, taking from your bodies your stony hearts and giving you natural hearts. I will put my Spirit within you and make you live by my statutes, careful to observe my decrees. You shall live in the land I gave your fathers; you shall be my people, and I will be your God."

That is the promise of Pentecost.

Joel, the prophet, is the following stop on our heritage journey. He reveals the promise of a new pentecost. Joel 2:23: "And do you, O children of Zion, exult and rejoice in the Lord, your God! He has given you the teacher of justice." God has given you the teacher of justice. Let us talk a little about that passage. The Essene community and the Qumran community were waiting mysteriously for this teacher of justice to appear, just as they were waiting for the Messiah. This teacher of justice took on Messianic qualities, and of course, we all know who that teacher is. The one who said, "Call no one else teacher but me," Jesus. "He has made the rain come down for you, the early and the late rain as before. The threshing floors shall be full of grain and the vats shall overflow. And I will repay you for the years which the locust has eaten." In other words I will restore your prosperity. Chapter 3:1 follows "Then I will pour out my Spirit upon all mankind. Your sons and daughters shall prophesy," every one of them, "your old men shall dream dreams, your young men shall see visions; upon even servants and handmaids I will pour out my Spirit." Everybody will be a prophet. My Spirit will be upon the human race. That is what it means. We saw the teacher coming; we saw the Spirit poured out at Pentecost, which introduced the final and last stage of the world, the final days. It is all there; God the Father has given His Son and His Spirit; the plentitude is there. We are in the fullness of time! That is ordinarily what the last days mean. It is all there; there is no fourth person of the Blessed Trinity yet to come. It has all been poured out; the final act is on. The curtain is up.

Pentecost is the fulfillment of much of these prophecies. The 120 people at Pentecost suddenly became new men and new women. The Spirit came upon them. Just as the Spirit had overshadowed Mary and Jesus came alive in her; just as the Spirit came upon Jesus at the Jordan and empowered Him for ministry, so the Spirit came upon the 12 and the Church, the body of Christ, was born. The Spirit was in them and they knew it. They were being taught and guided by the Spirit. That is Pentecost.

An interesting thing about Pentecost is this: I do not know whether you ever understood this before, but remember what Jesus said about John the Baptist: "The least person in the kingdom is greater than John the Baptist."* What does that mean? It means the least person after Pentecost is greater than John the Baptist. Is that not amazing? You are greater than John the Baptist because you are living in the final act.

John did not know what the final act was going to be. Like all the prophets of the Old Testament, he was a man upon whom the Spirit came occasionally. The Spirit came to them on occasion, but you are baptized in the Holy Spirit. As a fish is in water, you are in the Holy Spirit. The Holy Spirit is your milieu. The Holy Spirit is similar to a 24-hour radio station that you can tune into at your leisure. You are in the realm of the Spirit. The least person living now after Pentecost is more fortunate than John the Baptist.

The last word I want to give you is John 14:23. Jesus said, "Anyone who loves me will be true to my word, and my Father will love him; and we will come to him and make our dwelling place within him. He who does not love me does not keep my words. This much have I told you while I was still with you; the Paraclete, the Holy Spirit whom the Father will send in my name, he will instruct you, he will teach you everything." That is E-V-E-R-Y-T-H-I-N-G! If you know your heritage, you can claim that. If you do not want that heritage, you can go back to cheese sandwiches, bread and cheese. "He will instruct you in everything and remind you of all that I told you. So my peace I give you." From now on, if you lack wisdom, if you lack this heritage, know that it belongs to you. Ask for it, and it will be given to you; ask and it will be given to you in abundance.

*Matthew 11:11

CHAPTER 4

Need for Wisdom in the Renewal

Today we have a tremendous need for wisdom, particularly in the renewal. One reason is that often when we are at the crossroads we come to impasses; we do not know which direction to take, this way or that way. Should I pursue community or parish renewal; should I be with this group or that group; should I move there or stay here? There are many important decisions we need to make, crucial decisions. It reminds me of Solomon and the prayer he said when he saw the mass of people and that great kingdom he inherited from his father, David. He prayed, "Who can rule this mass of people, Lord. Give me wisdom so I can rule it as you would have me rule it."[1] It is a prayer we all should say. Lord, as things are getting more complex, as the situation begins to stagger our imagination and confound our reason, grant us wisdom. We really need wisdom. I think wisdom is the most valuable gift in the renewal today. That is why I felt inspired to write about it.

You all know that according to Scripture, God has a plan. We call that plan "Providence." We Christians have lost our concept of "Providence," which was incidentally a very key idea in the early history of this country. All it means, if you reflect upon it, is God being a Father, the Father planning, the Father foreseeing. The Latin "providere" means to see ahead and provide for; that is what "Providence" is. God sees ahead, provides for and has a plan. He has a plan for His church. Read about His plan; it is described beautifully in Ephesians 1. He has a plan for you as an individual; He has a plan for your family; He has a plan for each of your children; He has a plan for your community, for your prayer group. God's plan is "Providence." Wisdom for us is to discover God's plan and to move with it. It is one thing to know His will, to have a view of it today. Next week, however, you may have lost sight of part of it, perhaps thinking you have grasped it completely, only to find you are doing your thing and God's plan is a little different from what you expected; thus, you have lost sight of it.

Let me give you an example. Suppose Jesus, the Good Shepherd, or the Pied Piper, came here in person, in the flesh, and said, "Come on, you 300 people, come on with me, get into your cars. We are going down to the interstate." We would all get into our cars and follow Jesus down the interstate, the big highway. We would be going along, "la, de, da," and in conversation with one another. We would not necessarily know where we were going, but we would be following Jesus. Suddenly Jesus takes a detour off the interstate down a little byway. The car behind Him does not particularly notice Him, so the whole troop is still going down the interstate, and Jesus is in some other city! That is why I say wisdom is to know

God's plan, to obey it and to be able to move with it day by day, hour by hour, minute by minute. Sometimes He changes or seems to change plans from morning to night. If, for example, you are dealing with a person who needs repentance in the morning and the person repents at noontime — He would give you a different word at night for that person. You have to really stay with the Lord and see what He is doing and move with Him. Wisdom is that ability to know God's plan and to move with it, to obey it. Take His hand and do not let go; do not think you know; do not depend upon yourself. Many prayer groups, I think, have got a vision, a great vision; they think they know. They have that vision and they are going to fulfill it come what may, even if their numbers dwindle and dwindle and there is nobody left! Meantime God is in another town. Wisdom is the belief that God has a plan and the ability to discover that plan in prayer. You get a glimpse of it and then you move with it, day by day, hour by hour. That is what wisdom is.

Perhaps I can illustrate this point through an experience of my own just before I came into the renewal in the terrible sixties. I was teaching in a college seminary and things were going badly. The numbers were going down every year. There were strikes and rebellions and all kinds of problems here, so characteristic of the college circles in the sixties. One net result for me was that I began to pray much more. Prior to that I was very busy working, trying to implement Vatican II, until things began to go sour. They began to go downhill; my friends were leaving the priesthood. Others whom you could count on, the laity, who would always have been there, suddenly were not. Then I began to pray, really pray. I prayed to God that He would begin renewing the seminary, that He would begin really getting the Cursillo movement on fire and He would have the Search movement catch on in every city and town and build up His post-Vatican II communities as He gave us an initial vision He was going to do. I began to pray. You know what happened? The more I prayed the worse things got! They got worse and they got worse; I prayed more and more, and everytime I prayed it was like God was simply shaking His head and saying "No!"

What did I learn from all that? Well, first of all this experience led me to the Baptism in the Holy Spirit. That alone was like going from BC to AD. One thing I learned was this. That no matter how long I prayed, God was not about to buy my plan! We are all pretty good at making plans, are we not? Then we try to sell them to God. That is what our prayers often are. We make plans and try to sell them to God.

For example, twenty or thirty years ago the common sense, practical thinking of the whole church was that you built schools and you built novitiates. There seemed to be a boom. So, we built all kinds of schools, novitiates, seminaries. Do you realize that some of them were never used? Maybe God said, "Well, I did not tell you to build them." We had grasped a vision twenty to thirty years ago; we were going down the highway, "la, de, da," and God had gone off the byroad and we did not even notice it! We were not listening to the prophets. We did not even believe much in prophecy in those days. We did not believe we could really come into, tap into, God's plan. So, we built all kinds of new buildings and then had to close many of them. I used to pray, "Oh, Lord, when are you going to start doing such and such?" And nothing would happen. Now, years later, my prayer is entirely different. My prayer is more like this: "Oh, Lord, please slow down and let me catch my breath." I think you have experienced that feeling too. God is so far ahead of us. He is not behind us. God is so far ahead of us — the secret is to get on his wavelength. When you are finally on His wavelength, it is — "whoosh" — like lightning; everything works, nothing fails. Even your crosses and crucifixions all lead to resurrection. That is the promise of Scripture. In Romans 8:28, Paul concludes from his experience that "For to those who love God, who are called in His plan, everything works for good." You no longer draw a single wasted breath. Everything builds, even your failures. Is that not tremendous insurance? Where can you beat that? What a promise.

Once I learned that, it turned my life right around; I did not have to make plans and sell them to God; rather I was able to humbly discover with others and in personal prayer, what God's plan was and say "yes" to it and move with it. How fast things happen when you get a group of people doing that! The reason, you see, is that God is more interested in renewing this world than we are. You do not have to twist His arm and say, "Come renew my neighborhood; or come renew my town." He has been wanting to renew these places before we were born! If we get on His wavelength, He will do it, and do it so fast we will be amazed. But the secret is to get on His wavelength, to catch His plans and to move with Him. It may be in strange ways sometimes that things happen, but they will happen. Wisdom will guide you and wisdom will be the key to God's plan.

There is a beautiful section in Psalm 33 about the Father's plan that illustrates the example I just shared with you of my own frustrations. In verse 10, it reads, "The Lord brings to nought the plans of nations; he foils the designs of peoples. But the plan of the Lord stands forever." It is like rock. "The design of his heart, through all generations. Happy the people whose God is the Lord. The people he has chosen for his own inheritance." Verse 18, "See, the eyes of the Lord are upon those who fear him," who are looking to Him, in other words. "The eyes of the Lord are upon those who hope for his kindness. To deliver them from death and preserve them even in spite of famine." In other words, even in death and in famine, God will take care of His own. If we are on His wavelength, we have nothing to worry about. We are going to ride right into eternity. What a promise! The plan of the Lord stands forever.

You know what is going on in the church right now? It is like a big shakedown. God is shaking the tree and as Hebrews says, "Everything that God has not planted will come down."[2] There are many things "coming down" in the church today. One of the big things God is doing in His church is tearing down the things He never built up. I say. "Alleluia." It hurts sometimes because we are pretty attached to them, but the things that He never planned, He is tearing down. Things that He has built, if they have moved with Him (and sometimes they have not; sometimes they are still on the super highway going to their spiritual death) will be fine. The things He has planned last forever into eternity. This thought is very consoling if you grasp it — the plan of a loving father.

What else does that psalm say? First, He has a plan and it lasts forever, and secondly it is a plan of His heart. It is a plan of love. It is a loving plan from a loving Daddy. This psalm is always used on the feast of the Sacred Heart. It used to be known as the Sacred Heart Psalm. The loving Father loving His children — if you grasp it, you could meditate on it forever. The third thing that that psalm says about the plan of God is that He frustrates other plans. He frustrates the designs of the other nations. He frustrates the plans of prayer groups, parishes, even bishops, which are not from Him. He frustrates them. He lets them die.

Let us take a look at the Spirit, and then we will come to Jesus briefly. This passage applies to the Holy Spirit and there is some great light for us in it — Wisdom 7 starting with verse 22. It is a passage where Solomon prays for and receives wisdom along with an abundance of riches. You see, when you receive wisdom in the Bible, everything else comes besides. Solomon prayed for wisdom and God gave him everything else he never dared pray for, because "he hit the jackpot." He prayed for the right thing. God gave him everything else besides. In Wisdom 7:22, Solomon says, "Such things as are hidden I learned, and such as are plain; for Wisdom, the artificer of all, taught me."

Now look at his beautiful description of the Holy Spirit who is our wisdom.

"[He] is a spirit intelligent, holy, unique,
"Manifold, subtle, agile, clear, unstained, certain,
"Not baneful, loving the good, keen, unhampered, beneficent, kindly,
"Firm, secure, tranquil, all-powerful, all-seeing,
"And pervading all spirits, though they be intelligent, pure and very subtle.
"For Wisdom is mobile beyond all motion, and she penetrates and pervades all things by reason of her purity.
"For she is an aura of the might of God and a pure effusion of the glory of the Almighty; therefore nought that is sullied enters into her.
"For she is the refulgence of eternal light, the spotless mirror of the power of God, the image of his goodness.
And she, who is one, can do all things, and renews everything while herself perduring;
"And passing into holy souls from age to age, She produces friends of God and prophets."

That is what is happening in the renewal now. The Holy Spirit, Wisdom, is passing into holy souls and producing friends of God and prophets. It is the work of the Spirit in wisdom.

"For there is nought God loves, be it not one who dwells with Wisdom
"For she is fairer than the sun and surpasses every constellation of the stars.
"Compared to light, she takes precedence; for that, indeed, night supplants, but wickedness prevails not over Wisdom.
"Indeed, she reaches from end to end mightily and governs all things well."

Wisdom governs the world. So, Solomon says, "Her I loved and sought after from my youth. I sought to take her for my bride and was enamored of her beauty." I wanted to get married to this Spirit, is what he is saying. "She adds to nobility the splendor of companionship with God; ever the Lord of all loved her." Now, here are two gifts that are fantastic: "For she is instructress in the understanding of God, and the selector of his works." You want to know which work to do, "A" or "B"? You want a "Rayma" on which work to get into? There is the promise. "And if riches be a desirable possession in life, what is richer than Wisdom, who produces all things?"[3] Also, "If one yearns for copious learning, she knows the things of old, and infers those yet to come. She understands the turns of phrases and the solutions of riddles; signs and wonders she knows in advance and the outcome of times and ages."[4] So he concludes his prayer: "And so I went to the Lord and besought him, and said with all my heart," Lord, give me wisdom. That is the Spirit, the Father and His plan, the Spirit who tells us how to select even among the various good things that are in front of us. Wisdom is the instructress of everything.

Now, a word about Jesus. There are a couple of lines in I Corinthians 1:30, that provided a whole philosophy for Abbot Columba Marmion of Maredsous Abbey in Belgium. Many will remember the famous school of spirituality that was associated with Abbot Marmion. He got it all from this one verse. "God the Father made Christ to be our wisdom and sanctification and justification." God made Jesus to be our wisdom! By our union with Him, our bridal union with Jesus, we come into Wisdom. The Spirit of Jesus comes into us. Intimate union with Jesus produces wisdom, through the Eucharist, through prayer. I will write more about this idea later, but I felt that you should be given a trinitarian expression of wisdom even if at this point it had to be a short one.

[1] Kings 3:9
[2] Hebrews 12:26
[3] Wisdom 8:4
[4] Wisdom 8:8

CHAPTER 5

Good and Bad Biblical Examples of Wisdom

I would like now to go through some biblical bad examples of human wisdom and then give you some good examples of divine wisdom. First we will look at King Saul. He was chosen by the Lord and by Samuel the prophet to be anointed as the first king of Israel. God had great plans for him. He was truly anointed and empowered by the Holy Spirit. Look at I Samuel 10:6; Samuel said to Saul, "The Spirit of the Lord will rush upon you, and you will join these others in their prophetic state and you will be changed into another man." That sounds almost like something we say in the fifth session of the Life in the Spirit Seminar. As Saul left Samuel, God gave him "another heart." In other words God equipped him. "That very day all these signs came to pass. When they were going from there to Gibeah, a band of prophets met him, and the Spirit of God rushed upon him so that he joined them in their prophetic state." There is no question about his being anointed by the Spirit for the job of being king of Israel!

But what did he do after his anointing? Not too much, I'm afraid. I am just going to give you some examples of how Saul lost the Spirit, how he kept on the highway and did not go down the byroad with Christ. Israel was doing battle with the Philistines; Saul, the king, was not supposed to offer sacrifice. That was Samuel the priest's role. This was a very rigid law in Israel and Samuel said, "you wait, I will get there and we will have the sacrifice." But the battle was about to begin, Samuel was a little late. What happened was this:

> "Saul waited seven days — the time Samuel had determined. When Samuel did not arrive at Gilgal, the men began to slip away from Saul. He then said, 'Bring me the holocaust and peace offerings,' and he offered up the holocaust.
> "He had just finished this offering when Samuel arrived. Saul went out to greet him, and Samuel asked him, 'What have you done?' Saul replied: 'When I saw that the men were slipping away from me, since you had not come by the specified time, and with the Philistines assembled at Michmash, I said to myself, Now the Philistines will come down against me at Gilgal, and I have not yet sought the Lord's blessing. So in my anxiety I offered up the holocaust.' Samuel's response was: 'You have been foolish! Had you kept the command the Lord your God gave you, the Lord would now establish your kingship in Israel as lasting; but as things are, your kingdom shall not endure. The Lord has sought out a man after his own heart.'"[1]

The next example is in Chapter 15. The Israelites are now going to do battle against Amalek, Samuel said to Saul:

> "It was I the Lord sent to anoint you king over his people Israel. Now, therefore, listen to the

message of the Lord. This is what the Lord of Hosts has to say. 'I will punish what Amalek did to Israel when he barred his way as he was coming up from Egypt. So, go now attack Amalek and deal with him and all that he has under the ban. Do not spare him, but kill men and women, children and infants, oxen and sheep, camels and asses.' "[1]

The above ideas seem a little primitive to us. Old Testament morality was not quite up to New Testament standards, but the idea behind all of this was that they were so afraid of contamination, of idolatry, that usually they would go into a city or a town and instead of being influenced, as they often were, by the idolatry of that city, the prophets would urge that the whole city be destroyed, everything in it. That is the nature of the command of the Lord that was quoted here. Now, what did Saul do with this command? He went into battle and won. However:

"He took Agag, the king, alive, but on the rest of the people he put into effect the ban of destruction by the sword. He and his troops spared Agag and the best of the fat sheep and oxen, and the lambs. But they refused to carry out the doom on anything that was worthwhile, dooming only what was worthless and of no account.

"Then the Lord spoke to Samuel: 'I regret having made Saul king, for he has turned from me and has not kept my command . . . . When Samuel came to him, Saul greeted him: 'The Lord bless you! I have kept the command of the Lord!' (We won, basically.) But Samuel asked 'What then is the meaning of this bleating of sheep that comes to my ears, and the lowing of oxen that I hear?' Saul replied, 'They were brought from Amalek. The men spared the best sheep and oxen to sacrifice to the Lord, your God, but we have carried out the ban on the rest.' Samuel said to Saul: 'Stop! Let me tell you what the Lord said to me last night.' 'Speak!' he replied. Samuel then said: 'Though little in your own esteem, are you not leader of the tribes of Israel? The Lord anointed you king of Israel and sent you on a mission saying 'Go and put the sinful Amalekites under a ban of destruction. Fight against them until you have exterminated them. Why then have you disobeyed the Lord? You have pounced on the spoil, thus displeasing the Lord.' Saul answered Samuel: 'I did indeed obey the Lord and fulfill the mission on which the Lord sent me. I have brought back Agag, and I destroyed Amalek under the ban. But from the spoil the men took sheep and oxen, the best of what had been banned, to sacrifice to the Lord their God in Gilgal.' "[2]

But Samuel said these famous lines,

"Does the Lord so delight in holocausts and sacrifices as in obedience to the command of the Lord?

"Obedience is better than sacrifice, and submission than the fat of rams.

"For a sin like divination is rebellion and presumption is the crime of idolatry."[3]

Put that in your pipe and smoke it! "But I thought . . . !" Did you ever hear someone say, "But I thought . . . !" "But I thought this would please the Lord!" The Lord said, "Presumption is the crime of idolatry." That is strong, is it not? "Because you have rejected the command of the Lord, he too has rejected you as ruler." As for Saul, he goes downhill from there on. He ends up in witchcraft, a murderer, trying to kill

David, jealous. He just gets destroyed. This man, Saul, who was once filled with the Spirit, is completely destroyed.

I would like to draw your attention to a particular passage in the New Testament. It is in Galatians; you may not have noticed it before, Galatians 3:1, where Paul says:

> "You foolish Galatians, you senseless Galatians, who has cast a spell over you — before whose eyes Jesus Christ was displayed to view upon his cross? I want to learn only one thing from you; how did you receive the Spirit? Was it through observance of the law or through faith in what you heard? How could you be so stupid? After beginning in the Spirit, are you now to end it in the flesh? Have you had such remarkable experiences, all to no purpose?"[4]

It is important for you to remember that the Galatians had tremendous charismatic experiences. They had been baptized in the Holy Spirit. "Have you had such tremendous experiences, all to no purpose — if indeed they were to no purpose? Is it because you observe the law or because you have faith in what you have heard that God lavishes the Spirit on you and works wonders in your midst?' " All right now, what happened there? The Galatians started in the Spirit and then they became like Saul. They meant well, they wanted to bring in the Jews. They wanted to gather the whole synagogue together, and so, like Saul, they said, "We thought that by going back to the synagogue, in keeping the law and getting into our synagogues, we would bring the whole thing together.

We thought that by embracing the law we would gather all our Jewish people together and we would be one." We thought! Paul says, "You fools, you senseless Galatians, you presumed that and what happened? I no longer see evidence among you of the gifts of the Spirit. All you have is law again. You have gone back into law. You started with the Spirit and you are back in the law." And that, my brothers and sisters, sometimes is happening today, with people, for example, attempting on their own to get into parish renewal rather than keeping faithful to the initial anointing of the Holy Spirit with all His power upon their lives. We are doing what the foolish Galatians did, sometimes unwittingly. I will expand on that idea a little later. That is what the foolish Galatians were doing. They were going backward instead of forward and they *thought* that they were advancing Christ's cause, just as Saul *thought* he was advancing God's cause. They were *presuming,* and what was actually happening was that they were making a terrible mistake. Paul had to come and castigate them. It was a bad example of starting with the Spirit and then losing the Spirit.

I see the same situation happening in many prayer groups. For example, in your prayer group, is the Spirit as much in evidence now as He was two, three, five or seven years ago? If not, might you not be "foolish Galatians"?

Let us take a look at some good examples now, some good examples of divine wisdom. The Galatians were full of human wisdom and lacking totally in divine wisdom. Someone told me of a great man of

God, preacher and healer, who while going through the hospital, would pray for a particular person and that person would be healed. He would, however, just shake hands with another person, he would call another to repentance, while he would just wave to still another as he continued along. Someone asked him once. "How come you do not pray over everybody? How come you just single out certain people?" His reply was, "You do not know anything about the healing ministry, my friend. The secret of the healing ministry is not the gift of healing. It is discernment on whom God wants to heal, and when." And so you discern that God wants to heal Charlie, call Mary to repentance, just say hello to Joe and so on.

I heard Ruth Stapleton give her own witness and in many ways it was very similar. It is a powerful example of what I am saying here. She learned wisdom through a lot of hard knocks, but I will just give you her conclusion. It was a long time after she initially received the gift of healing that God allowed her to use it. He put her through years of testing so that she could learn obedience to him. She made at the conclusion of her talk, addressing primarily those persons interested in the healing ministries, a very powerful statement. "There is no such thing as a healing ministry; there is only obedience to the Lord!" That is a very powerful statement indeed.

I would now like to contrast Saul with David. In order to do so, I will again make reference to the book of Samuel, from the Old Testament. Saul's replacement was David, a young boy. God chose youth to confound the strong, the foolish to confound the wise.

David is a man after God's own heart. I might point out that he was a bigger sinner than Saul was. When David sinned, he sinned! It is almost scandalous to read his story. He committed adultery with and married Bathsheba, after having her husband Uriah killed! But that is not the end of the world. We are all sinners. The important thing is having a heart for the Lord. David repented. He had a heart for the Lord. Saul could not have done that; David did. Here is an example of his letting the Lord be Lord. That is what wisdom is, letting God be God, letting the Lord's plans prevail. The situation we find in I Samuel 23, is David's being pursued by Saul, who has fallen from power and is trying to hold on to the kingdom by his human, desperate means. Saul is after David; he wants to kill him, and David is in hiding in the city of Keilah.

"David received information that the Philistines were attacking Keilah and plundering the threshing floors. So he consulted the Lord, inquiring, 'Shall I go and defeat these Philistines?' The Lord answered, 'Go, for you will defeat the Philistines and rescue Keilah.' But David's men said to him: 'We are afraid here in Judah. How much more so if we go to Keilah against the forces of the Philistines! Again David consulted the Lord, who answered, 'Go down to Keilah, for I will deliver the Philistines into your power.' (The second time David consulted the Lord) David then went with his men to Keilah and fought with the Philistines. He drove off their cattle and inflicted a severe defeat on them, and thus rescued the inhabitants of Keilah.

"Abiathar, son of Ahimelech, who had fled to David, went down with David to Keilah, taking the ephod with him."

The passage states that David consulted the Lord. What he was asking was, "Lord, give me a 'Rayma.' What do I do?" Let us take a look in the Old Testament at how David appealed to God for guidance. He did it through the use of this mysterious but effective tool called the ephod. What is the ephod? If you want to read about its origin, you can find it in Exodus 29:5. The ephod was this. It was the formula that God gave to Israel for determining His will in certain instances. It became the property of the high priest when he was vested. He put an ephod similar to the humeral veil over his shoulders. It was like a little cape. In it was a little pocket called the breastpiece, and in the breastpiece were two dice. One was called the Urim, the "yes" die; the other the Thummin, the "no" die. The ephod was to be worn by the high priest and used on behalf of Israel, when its people needed to know which way to go. "Do we stay on the highway?" "Do we take the byroad?" What they would do was this. They would go to the temple and offer sacrifice. Then the high priest would ask, after worship, after deep union with God, "do we fight today or not?" That is the reason David brought the high priest along with him; the high priest carried the ephod. David always asked the Lord; Saul did not. That is the difference between the one man and the other. Not that one man was a sinner and the other was not. They were both sinners, but David let God be God. David was content to be assistant general, to let God be the general. You can find example after example of that idea throughout the Old Testament. Let us continue now with I Samuel 23:7:

"When Saul was told that David had entered Keilah, he said: 'God has put him in my grip. Now he has shut himself in, for he has entered a city with gates and bars.' Saul then called all the people to war, in order to go down to Keilah and besiege David and his men. When David found out that Saul was planning to harm him, He said to the priest Abiathar, 'Bring forward the ephod.' David then said, 'O Lord God of Israel, your servant has heard a report that Saul plans to come to Keilah, to destroy the city on my account. Will they hand me over? Will Saul come down as your servant has heard?' The Lord answered, 'He will come down.' (The Urim die came out) David then asked, 'Will the citizens of Keilah deliver me and my men into the grasp of Saul?' and the Lord answered, 'Yes.' So David and his men, about six hundred in number, left Keilah and wandered from place to place."

In other words, in this particular case they did not fight. In one instance they fought; here they did not fight. God said that if you fight, you will be defeated. You will be betrayed. David was saved by wisdom. The Bible talks much about being saved by wisdom.

Another example in the same book relates that while David was at war, his family, relatives and friends, as well as the families of all his soldiers, were taken captive in Ziklag, by an enemy. While the men were fighting wars, their families were captured. Therefore, the men were ready to stone David. The story is told I Samuel 30:6.

"Now David found himself in great difficulty, for the men spoke of stoning him, so bitter were they over the fate of their sons and daughters. But with renewed trust in the Lord his God, David said to Abiathar, the priest, son of Ahimelech, 'Bring me the ephod!' When Abiathar brought him the ephod, David inquired of the Lord, 'Shall I pursue these raiders? Can I overtake them?' The Lord answered him, 'Go in pursuit, for you shall surely overtake them and effect a rescue.'"

David did as the Lord directed; he won. God was with him. He got his whole family back as well as the families of his men. From these examples you see the kind of man David was. If David lived in our time, he would be singing, "Jesus is Lord!" all the time. He would be saying with John the Baptist, "May He increase and I decrease." That is the kind of man David was. He loved the Lord; that is why David wrote psalms. Also he was not afraid to make a fool of himself before the people of Israel, dancing before the Ark. His wife said, "What a fool you are." She was cursed by the Lord and made barren for the rest of her life for that. David was blessed because he loved the Lord. He sinned, but he repented. He loved the Lord; he danced for Him; he wrote songs for Him; he played before Him, and most of all, he obeyed him. Therefore, under David, the conquest of the promised land occurred. It was the fulfillment of the promise made to Abraham. This is the only time in history that Jerusalem was considered to be the greatest city in the world. Jerusalem became the capital of the world only under David. With the leadership of David, who allowed the Lord to be Lord, Jerusalem reached its apogee. Solomon let it go downhill because he lost the wisdom he originally had. Remember the words from Deuteronomy, "The Lord was their leader."[5] This was true with David; the Lord alone was leading Israel. And when He was leading them, He brought Israel to its fulfillment; Jerusalem became the capital of the world; everybody from the ends of the earth wanted to come to Jerusalem, including the Queen of Sheba. David was a man of wisdom; he let God be God; he could say "yes" to God's plan.

Let us take a look at an excerpt from the New Testament, Acts 16:6. Here is a beautiful example of letting the Lord lead. In this passage Paul and Silas were traveling on a missionary journey. "They next traveled through Phrygia and Galatian territory because they had been prevented by the Holy Spirit from preaching the message in the province of Asia." Their first impulse had been to go into Asia; however, somehow or other the Holy Spirit had given them a "Rayma" saying, "No." They were thus prevented by the Holy Spirit from going where they had first intended. Had Paul used "common sense," he might have said, "It is common sense that we go to Asia; God gave us our common sense, our human reason; therefore, we have got to use our reason and go to Asia." He would have asked God to bless his common sense, but blessed or not, had he followed his common sense, he would have been defeated in Asia. Paul and Silas did not do this, however; they followed the Spirit which prevented them from teaching the message in the province of Asia. "When they came to Mysia, they tried to go on into Bithynia, but again the

Spirit of Jesus would not allow them." Just like David, Paul and Silas consulted the Lord and the Spirit said, "No. Jesus had promised that the Spirit will guide you in everything."

> "Crossing through Mysia instead, they came down to Troas. There one night Paul had a vision. A man of Macedonia stood before him and invited him, 'Come over to Macedonia and help us.' After this vision, we immediately made efforts to get across to Macedonia, concluding that God had summoned us to proclaim the good news there."

Instead of going into Bithynia, Paul and Silas, led by the Spirit, went into Europe. Can you imagine that, my brothers and sisters? That is how the gospel came to Europe, from where it came to us — through a vision! What would your superior say to you, or what would your bishop say to you if you said, "Well, I had a vision to go to Africa." That is how the gospel came to Europe, through a vision, and look what happened. Quickly I will tell you the story. Paul and Silas go into Philippi and they meet Lydia and some women at the river bank. They begin a little prayer meeting and all is going well until they run into serious trouble with a girl who has a spirit of divination. Satan poses a tremendous obstacle and the first thing you know, they are thrown into jail in Philippi, put into the stocks. They were beaten and then they were placed in the maximum security section of the jail, their mission seemingly "a bust." In reality, however, they were at Calvary, which is a good place to be. Now you and I, if we were Silas, would probably have said to Paul, "Paul, are you sure you had a vision!" But

Paul and Silas did not doubt the Holy Spirit for a moment. Actually, while they were in jail in Philippi, they were praising God. They were in the stocks; however, they were still praising God at midnight. Like Jesus, they never deviated one moment from the will of God. They were saying "yes"; they were hanging onto the Cross. They never asked any questions, never murmured as the Israelites did in the desert. They simply let themselves be guided by the Spirit. Therefore, they were content to praise God and sing hymns in jail. Then, in the middle of that night, God sent an earthquake. The jail opened, and probably it was the only town in history ever to be evangelized so quickly! You see how God's Wisdom, crazy as it may seem to us at times, works.

Let me close this section by sharing one of my experiences at Saint Patrick's. For about a month our pastoral team kept getting one word from the Lord, over and over again. Every time we had a meeting the Lord would say just one thing to us. He would say it in many different ways, but the underlying thought was consistently the same. What He would say was, "Get wisdom, get wisdom." We kept answering, "What do you mean, Lord?" His reply was, "Get wisdom." We would return the next week to pray again, and again He would say, "Get wisdom." This went on for about a month. Finally, we prayed and fasted for about a week and then we said, "Lord, what do you mean? You keep telling us to get wisdom. We have heard that; tell us something else." When we asked Him what He meant after we had prayed and fasted for it, do you know what He told us? He said,

"What I mean for you is this. Ask me everything; presume nothing. Take nothing for granted. Let me be the Lord in every one of your decisions." When we finally grasped what He meant, He continued to guide us in other ways.

[1] I Samuel 13:8-14
[2] I Samuel 15:8-21
[3] I Samuel 15:22-23
[4] Galatians 3:1-5
[5] Deuteronomy 32:12

CHAPTER 6

Contemplative Wisdom-Seeking

Before I expand upon the experience I mentioned at the end of the previous chapter about the Lord speaking to our group at Saint Patrick's concerning the acquisition of wisdom, I want to point out to you an interesting passage dealing with wisdom-seeking. This passage exemplifies, as did the examples given in the foregoing chapter, God's people asking Him to give them guidance through His Word. I Maccabees 3:44-48, is an example of the antiquity of the custom of asking the Lord for a "Rayma."

"The assembly gathered together to prepare for battle and to pray and implore mercy and compassion. Jerusalem was uninhabited, like a desert; not one of her children entered or came out. The sanctuary was trampled on, and foreigners were in the citadel; it was a habitation of Gentiles. Joy had disappeared from Jacob, and the flute and the harp were silent.

"Thus they assembled and went to Mizpah near Jerusalem, because there was formerly at Mizpah a place of prayer for Israel. That day they fasted and wore sackcloth; they sprinkled ashes on their heads and tore their clothes. They unrolled the scroll of the law, to learn about the things for which the Gentiles consulted the images of their idols."

What were they doing? They were seeking a "rayma" in the Word of God. They did not have a Bible, but they unrolled the Scroll to a point led by God's Spirit. They were seeking wisdom by using the Word of God. "Do we battle or not?" The Lord said, "Yes." They did battle, and they won! This, you can see, is an Old Testament example of the Lord giving guidance through Scripture. In this example, as in others, we see persons seeking guidance from the Lord in a solemn context of prayer and fasting in the community that was being assembled.

As I have previously mentioned, for about a month the Lord kept telling our community at Saint Patrick's, "Get wisdom." We did not understand what He meant. "Get wisdom; seek wisdom" was all He would communicate to us. When we did pray and fast and seek a meaning of what "get wisdom; seek wisdom," meant, the Lord told us, "This is what I mean. You are to ask Me everything. You are to take nothing for granted. You are to presume nothing. I want to be Lord. I want to be the head of this community. I want to make the decisions. Let Me make the decisions; that, for you, is wisdom. If you have any questions, ask Me. Ask Me everything. I will tell you the answers." That is what we learned, charismatically, was wisdom for us. I am not saying we were always faithful in asking the Lord everything, but that incident was a dramatic lesson for all of us. One of the reasons I am writing this book is that I believe that the Lord wants the message He gave to us to be disseminated to the Christian community at large. Proverbs 4:7 states it succinctly. "The beginning of wisdom is: get wisdom; at the cost of all you have, get understanding."

When the Lord can be Lord, things happen. Often, we think we have made the Lord our Lord; we think we have made Jesus our Lord and that we have put Him into the driver's seat of our life. We start singing with new meaning, "Jesus Is Lord." But even after we believe we have given Jesus dominion over all the areas of our life, we often find that, however inadvertantly, we have failed to seek His Wisdom in certain instances. I think perhaps we have abandoned too quickly the song, "Jesus Is Lord." We used to sing that song frequently a few years ago. It would be nice if we returned to it more often today. Once in prayer, while the whole group was singing "Jesus Is Lord," I heard the Lord say to me, "Am I?" Each time I hear that song now I hear the words from the Lord — "Am I?" Is He Lord of your marriage? Is He Lord of your relationship with each of your children? Is He Lord of your activities in your parish? Is He Lord of your work? Is He Lord of your prayer life? Is He Lord of your recreational life? Is He Lord of this phase and that phase of your life? Is He Lord of your block? All these are areas in which He wants to extend His Providence.

Wisdom is the path by which He will lead you. It is the path by which He will really become Lord as He was Lord for David. He wants to become Lord for you as He wants to become Lord of this renewal. The renewal has done great things, but if Jesus could truly be

78

the Lord of every phase in the renewal, it would be a hundred times as large as it is today. This passage from Proverbs reinforces what I am saying. It is a very strong passage similar to the type of Word He was giving us at Saint Patrick's. Proverbs 1:20-23:

> "Wisdom cries aloud in the street, in the open squares she raises her voice; down the crowded ways she calls out, at the city gates she utters her words: 'How long, you simple ones, will you love inanity, how long will you turn away at my reproof? Lo! I will pour out to you my spirit, I will acquaint you with my words."

"Wisdom cries," in some versions, "Wisdom screams, how long will you love emptiness . . . Lo! I want to pour out my spirit." God is saying, "Can you not hear Me. I am knocking at your door. I want to pour out wisdom, I want to bring you under the fountain of wisdom, My children. But, I often call and you do not hear Me. I extend My hand and no one takes it." That is what God is saying; God is screaming out His invitation to wisdom. The Bible is screaming, "Get wisdom."

Historical reflection is a characteristic of one who is seeking wisdom. The statement has been made that by not learning the mistakes of the past, we are condemned to repeat them. Not to learn from humanity's previous mistakes is to condemn yourself to suffer the folly of all who have erred throughout history; therefore, one of the things the wise man does is learn his ancestry. Many of the difficulties in the renewal as well as the problems with fundamentalist Bible scholarship today, stem from the fact that many have severed their connections with history. They have lost interest in how the Spirit has spoken throughout history; they have failed to hear his voice in all the wisdom of the fathers of the Church, in all the Bible scholars down through the ages. It is not as if God has been silent for centuries and we suddenly realize wisdom that nobody else ever had. Humility fits into this aspect of our search for wisdom as well. One of the paths to wisdom is humility; it takes humility to recognize and accept that you need to learn history, that you need to respect what your Father did in preparing the way for you.

One aspect of wisdom always in evidence in the history of the Church is that it is connected with, interwoven with, prayer. The way to find wisdom, as wisdom is screaming, is to be still before the Lord. In the stillness of your heart, you will hear God screaming. Psalm 46 states, "Be still before the Lord and wait."[1] Traditionally in the midst of renewal there has always been a combination of wisdom and contemplation. Saint Dominic coined the phrase, "The active apostolate is 'contemplata trodera,'" which means to hand on to others what you have heard in the stillness of prayer, to hand on what you have contemplated, to hand on to others what you have heard God say.

This process of handing on what you have heard is similar to going into a huddle on a football team where Jesus is the quarterback. You hear His signals and you carry them out. Often the Christian Church today, the Christian prayer group, is like a football team with eleven quarterbacks. No one can be still to hear the real quarterback. On God's football team, God the

Father is the coach; the quarterback is in perfect coordination with the Coach, even more highly coordinated with him than Dallas' Roger Staubach was with Tom Landry; the quarterback of God's football team is Jesus. He is the quarterback and the Holy Spirit is the means of communication used between the coach and the quarterback. The instinctive response of all the players on God's team is to know the mind of the coach and the mind of the quarterback by communicating with the Spirit. The plan of the Father is touchdown, touchdown, touchdown. That is how the Christian team should work. Unfortunately that does not seem to be the way it is working. Instead of the losses the Christian team has been suffering, there should be gains. The Christian team has the super star. God does not get beaten! We should never lose. We may go to Calvary and suffer some, but that is part of the game plan. If you are proceeding in wisdom, the greatest victory comes after Calvary which itself is part of the victory.

Saint Dominic and Saint Francis developed as contemplative disciples first and then they went out into the active apostolate. We in the Church today have forgotten that combination. We still have contemplative orders and we have active orders but there are tremendous weaknesses on both sides. Today contemplative orders, as well as active orders are perishing or diminishing, and one of the reasons is that there has been a great divorce between both wisdom-seeking and contemplation on the one hand, and between wisdom-seeking and activity on the other. The marriage has to take place again! There needs to be as close a relationship between them as there was between Francis and Clare, or between Dominic and his sisters. They were aware of what he was doing and could pray for his apostolate and tell him: "Dominic, do not do this; do not do that; do not go here; do not go there." We need to have the day come when the Trappist and the Carmelite will tell us "do not say this, do not say that." If only the Bishop and the priests could go to the contemplatives and say, "This is what is happening in my diocese. These are the problems with which I need help. I need some answers. I need some wisdom. Will you help me get it?" Then the Body of Christ would be the Body of Christ, and Jesus would be Lord and the diocese would prosper. Today, they hardly know each other. As a result monasteries are often getting into all kinds of fascinations such as TM [Transcendental Meditation], and the like. Thus, the Body of Christ, right in its midst, is lanquishing and perishing. What is needed is the marriage of contemplation and activity!

Jesus in His own Person, Paul in his own person, Francis in his own person, and Dominic in his own person, were both contemplative and active. Saint Teresa of Avila once told her very active sisters who were busy founding places all over Spain that it was dangerous to go out evangelizing in preference to sitting at the feet of Jesus before the Blessed Sacrament. It is dangerous for us to go out evangelizing if we would rather not be sitting still with the Lord, sitting at the Master's feet and listening to Him. You are only safe when you have heard Him and He has sent you out. You should strive to have the same marriage with wisdom that existed in Jesus' life. Jesus did not pray for the fun of it. He did not pray just to give us an example. Jesus was truly human. He was truly flesh, as we are. Jesus had to pray. He had to pray to catch His Father's signals for the day. That is why He was out early in the morning. He might have been tired, but He had to get out there early in the morning and say, "Dad, what do You want to do today?"

The Father might say, "Go to the next town." Thus, when the apostles came out seeking Him saying, "They all want you back there in Capernaum." He would say, "I have got to go to the next town."

If you read the Scriptures, particularly the Gospel of Luke, you will see that at every moment Jesus was led by the Spirit. You will see that Jesus is sometimes "impelled" by the Spirit, or "driven" by the Spirit. Jesus was led by wisdom, led by the Spirit of Wisdom to do this, to do that, to go up to Jerusalem and so on. Remember Peter with his human wisdom saying, "Jesus, You must not go to Jerusalem. We are having great inroads here in Galilee." Jesus said, "Get behind me, Satan. Yours is human wisdom and you do not know the ways of God." Jesus combined wisdom and activity; every great apostle has. In the history of the Church, we have had communities aiding the apostles, contemplative orders aiding the active orders. Such wisdom means that God can be God with prayers taking the role of the cloud, the pillar of fire, the ephod theology as well as the "Rayma" theology.

I left Saint Patrick's about five years ago when our outreach was getting very extensive in the diocese and the Bishop put me in charge of a program, a diocesan program for renewal in the Spirit, a program of evangelization primarily for charismatics. A small body of people came with me, an intercessory body of people who wanted to recapture the Spirit to which I have just referred. We called this little ministry the Bethany Ministry of Prayer and Evangelization. Four intercessors who had been in the leadership of the intercessory group at Saint Patrick's and two other evangelists came along with me. The seven of us were formed into the one body. Bethany is a beautiful word that says, "rest with the Lord." It is a contemplative word; it is a word that connotes the coming aside of the Lord, your staying with the Lord, your entertaining Him.

One day in prayer, the Lord gave us a beautiful vision. In this vision I was pushing a wheelbarrow and in the wheelbarrow was the Ark of the Covenant. The two other evangelists were by my side and the four intercessors were behind wearing aprons and holding the aprons out as if they were picking up things. In the aprons were two things: a brick and a Bible. When we put it all together, what the vision meant was that we were then a kind of traveling ministry and we were building with the Word. We felt that the Lord was saying, "As you are carrying the Ark about, My Presence about, you will build with the Word. You will build My temple. You will move the Ark into a temple by building with the Word." Prayer and the Word, contemplation and activity, these are wisdom.

Today hardly any young persons look to Christianity for power because they have not found power or wisdom in Christians. Rather they are looking to drugs, Eastern religions, and TM; and yet the greatest power on earth we have right within us! We Christians are the bearers of the greatest power, the greatest wisdom on the earth; however, we have them pretty well hidden under a bushel basket, so to speak. Thus, our poor kids in universities, the seventy odd per cent who do not go to church, are looking elsewhere for wisdom and power.

Jesus is stirring Himself. His team has been losing too long. He is coming on the clouds with power and majesty to effect a change in the world, to effect a change of civilization, to bring to an end an era of human wisdom, the age of the so-called "enlightenment," the real Dark Ages of humanity. Jesus is coming to bring an end to that age of man whom the Renaissance said "was the measure of all things." He is coming on the clouds in Heaven; He is stirring Himself to bring an eschatological change. He is coming to bring an apocalyptic event, an end to an era, an era of man where Christianity has been losing. He is going to come in power as He came to Jerusalem in the year 70, to Rome in 313. He is going to come in power and wisdom through dedicated people. He is raising up who can follow Him. Perhaps, then, like Gideon, His followers will have only three hundred men. This situation will be similar to that stated in Isaiah 2, "Christianity will be the city on the mountain that all the nations will stream to and say, 'teach us.'"

* Psalm 46:10

CHAPTER 7

"Rayma" and Charismatic Discernment

Many people seem to fear asking the Lord for a "rayma." Some have commented to me that asking for a "rayma" sounds like a kind of Biblical roulette. I am sure there have been many abuses with "raymas." However, there are abuses with many things religious and non-religious! There are certainly many abuses with alcohol; yet the Bible states, "a little wine is good for the stomach's sake."[1] Asking for a word from the Lord is a very beautiful and very old tradition. I have given examples from the Old Testament of the people of Israel asking the Lord for a "Rayma." I am not advocating anything like Bibical roulette or magic. The "rayma" is a source of wisdom that can be fantastic and emancipating, not at all enslaving. God's Word is meant to set you free, not to bind you, and God's Word is for everybody.

It is quite possible that Satan has used the idea of a roulette image to try to keep Christians from being set free by the Word of God. Satan is referred to in the Bible as a liar and a deceiver. The three big strategies of Satan are to lie, to rob and to murder. He tries to kill the life of God in us. He can do this first by lying to us, then stealing away our heritage. I want to destroy a lie. If you have never asked the Lord to speak to you in Scripture because you are afraid of Bible roulette or something similar, you are being lied to. May the Lord destroy that lie, because you are being deprived of a fantastic source of wisdom! God inspired the writing of the Bible for all of us. The Holy Spirit lives in you and there is nothing He loves to do better than teach you His word Himself. The Holy Spirit loves to teach; if you give Him a chance to teach you, He will. Jesus said, "Call no one else teacher."[2] The Bible says that in the new covenant, "brother will not have to teach brother or kinsman his kinsman; all will know the Lord directly."[3] John 6 states, "You all will be taught by God."[4] If you are being deprived, through a lie, of letting the Spirit teach you or personally touch you, may that lie be destroyed by the Cross of Christ. Throw terms like "magic," "Biblical roulette" and "cracking the Bible" out of your vocabulary. Use these terms only when they are really referring to abuses. One should think this way: "Oh, how God loves me! He lives within me, and He speaks to me all the time."

While I was working with our seminarians, we frequently visited the state institutions. Everyone is aware of the poor conditions in institutions; the institution we visited was not an exception to the rule. There was a woman there who to this day stands out in my memory, a beautiful old suffering black lady who had been subjected to institutional life for quite some time. Although she lay there amidst much oppression, she was so very peaceful and remarkably joyful. The young seminarians could not help but feel and absorb her joy. She always had something spiritual to impart to them. She was always smiling, and happily she would say, "Listen to the Scripture the Lord gave me today." She knew God; she possessed God. She was able to lie there contentedly and peacefully because she had her Bible and she had her God; she knew that her God loved her and that He would speak to her every day. She would beam from ear to ear and share the Scripture she received that day. Often the Word she shared would zero right into the hearts of the young seminarians. She had truly child-like faith. "Unless you become like little children you can not enter the Kingdom."[5] That little old lady was one of the most beautiful children I have ever met — a child at the age of seventy-five or eighty, a little child who knew that the Lord loved her, who could go, through extreme adversity and still be the most gentle, loving person to the attendants and to all who were around her.

When I speak of a "rayma," I am speaking about faith; I am speaking about deep prayer. I am not talking about magic or roulette. Let me give you some rules about how to ask the Lord for a Word for you. First of all, never ask Him until you are in deep prayer, until you have a sense of His Presence, until you have stirred up the Spirit within you, until you are in faith. Once you are in deep prayer, once you have a sense of the Spirit, then you can say with Samuel, "Speak Lord, your servant is listening."[6] I always ask the Lord for a Word after Communion because if there is any deep moment of union, that is it. Not to ask the Lord for something when the Eucharist is within you is to miss an opportunity of receiving Jesus' love. But you have got to reach out, like the woman in the Bible who reached out and touched the hem of Christ's garment. Reaching out is faith. You must believe that He is right within you. You must believe He wants to minister to you. Then in that belief you reach out and say, "Lord, speak." In faith, in deep prayer, you ask the Lord to give you a "rayma." Another good time to pray for a Word would be after you have prayed a rosary and have been in deep contemplation of the mysteries of Jesus. Or, after you have been praying in tongues for a considerable amount of time. Or, as a priest, after you have prayed the breviary. Never end a deep prayer session without asking the Lord to speak a word.

God is love. What is the essence of love? The essence of love is communication. It is pretty near to heresy to believe that God is love and God lives within me, but He never communicates Himself to me! God is love and He communicates Himself! He wants to communicate Himself constantly to us. The Spirit is screaming, "Open your doors; open your gates. I am knocking, can you not hear Me? Let Me in. I want to give you My mind. I want to give you My heart. I want all My people to have My mind, My heart and My power. I want all the world to see that I live in My people."

I feel that I have learned more from people, like the woman I described in the institution, than from all the schools and books of theology I have studied. You can learn more from a person of deep faith no matter what their theology. Many Christians have known for years that power and wisdom are flowing through them. A man like Oral Roberts can say, "I know that I know that I know." A little like Saint Paul who said, "I know Him in whom I believe."

There must, however, be a word of caution. It can be extremely dangerous if you do not proceed out of a deep faith experience, not only is this crazy, but it can also be extremely dangerous. If you act unthinkingly, you can open yourself to the world of evil spirits, many of whom are out there waiting to have an opportunity to tempt and ensnare you. Satan can quote Scripture. He did it before Jesus. He can do it in your presence too and make it sound impressive. It is amazing how Satan can give you right-on passages, or what seem like truly appropriate statements until a person of real discernment comes along and unmasks them. So ask the Lord for a Word, for a "rayma," only in faith and deep prayer when you are protected by the Blood of Jesus; otherwise it can be very dangerous.

There are six points of charismatic discernment that can be very helpful in the process that I am writing about. The first point I have already begun to comment on: deep prayer, especially listening prayer wherein you let God speak. Deep prayer must be accompanied by expectant faith. If you do not expect God to do anything for you, He will not. Faith is the door, expectant faith. Jesus is knocking, but your faith has to open the door. Someone said that in our times it appears that we have added a ninth beatitude to the eight given us in the Gospel. "Blessed are they who expect nothing for they will not be disappointed!" Get into deep prayer, and then ask the Holy Spirit to answer your questions; He will do so. A bridal union with Jesus through deep prayer is the key. The Church is not called to be bridegroom. Jesus is the bridegroom. The Church is called to be bride! The image of the Church is bride; let Jesus be the bridegroom! Wisdom comes to the bride through deep union with the bridegroom. God made Jesus "to be our wisdom"[7] and by deep union with the bridegroom, by leaning on Him, looking toward Him, as Mary did, we become seats of wisdom.

The second point in charismatic discernment is that we need to pay more attention to the charismatic gifts of the Spirit. We need to use them; we need to sharpen them; we need to grow in them. Today, tragically, many prayer groups, many of those in the renewal, do not have the use of the gifts that they had in the beginning. I say tragically because if you read 1 Corinthians 14, carefully, Paul states that the gifts of the Spirit "build up the Church."[8] Why is the Church not being built up today? The tools God gave us are not being used! It seems that many people want the Church to be built, but they do not want the charismatic gifts; that is unfortunate, because if there are no gifts, there will be no building. In 1 Corinthians 14, Paul states, "Make love your aim, but seek the gifts of the Spirit." That is a command. That is a Scriptural command! A great deal of wisdom is being missed today by a great majority in the Church because the gifts are being bypassed. Further reinforcement of the need for the use of the gifts can be found in Proverbs, "a people without prophecy becomes demoralized."[9] We, God's own people are being demoralized today because we are not utilizing His gifts, especially that of prophecy. Some groups and individuals say, "Well, we are more mature now; we do not need the gifts of the Spirit." That is very dangerous; that is pride; we need them now more than ever! If we do not use the gifts, we will be going down that super highway I mentioned in an earlier chapter, while Jesus is on the byroad.

The gifts of the Spirit enable us to keep up with the Lord and His plan as it unfolds day by day. Individuals, as well as groups both large and small, from prayer groups to nations, need to use the gifts; a word of wisdom is necessary in one situation; a word of knowledge is important in another; prophecy is needed in some instances, and a "rayma" is important at still other times. It is the totality of the gifts of the Spirit that gives us the plan of the Lord. Our mission, perhaps our greatest mission in the renewal, is to restore to normal church life the tools for building the Church, and those tools are the gifts of the Holy Spirit.

The third point needed in charismatic discernment is to keep a journal. This journal need not be anything elaborate, just a pad, be it thick or thin; have it with you so that when the Lord speaks to you, you can make note of the "rayma." I never go around without a little pad in my pocket. This is old wisdom. Ignatius, for example, urged all of us to keep a journal; spiritual writers throughout the centuries have kept journals. When the Lord speaks to you, when you receive a "rayma," write it down.

I have been referring primarily to one privileged way the Lord speaks to us, that being through His Word, the Bible, for He is a teacher and loves to teach the Word He gave us. However, "raymas" come in many ways: through a Word you have received in Scripture, through a Word that has been spoken by a preacher or by a neighbor; through a circumstance in life, a dream, or a vision. God's Words are coming to us all the time in many varied fashions. Write down what God has been saying to you; it does not have to be lengthy; make it concise. The important point is that a journal be kept.

Every prayer group, every community should keep a journal or a log. No prayer group is just a prayer meeting. Have you not noticed that every prayer meeting, if it is well run, has a theme? God wants to say something; He wants to lay a building block in the wall that is being constructed. He sets a theme for prayer meetings. Note down those themes; they are part of the architecture of your community, part of His plan which is being revealed to you. Therefore, it is most important that you keep a log of the themes of your prayer group. Samuel reinforces this idea when he admonishes us not to let a single word of God drop to the ground. Every Word should become a building block; every prayer meeting should be a building block in the temple that God is constructing.

I remember sometimes we would come to impasses in our community and we would say, "Where do we go now? What do we do now?" Someone would always respond, "Let us take a look at the log!" When we went back two or three months and looked at our prayer meetings, looked at the pastoral team meetings, we would invariably say, "Ah! So!" It was not that God had not spoken; it was rather that we failed to hear what He had said.

The fourth point of charismatic discernment that I wish to stress is that the Word which you are hearing must be obeyed. In Hebrew the word for listen meant to hear and to obey. The two concepts were considered to be one. "Listen to my voice," meant both listen to it and obey it. With our "great" thinking we have dichotomized the Hebrew; we have one word for "hear" and another word for "obey." How did the wise man build his house on a rock? He built it by hearing the Word and putting it into practice. The foolish man heard the Word, but did not keep a journal. He forgot about all those prayer meetings, kept no records of the Words received; thus, the foolish man lost everything. When you hear the Word, obey it; put it into practice.

Some prayer groups are beautiful for this. Prophecy comes forth and they all obey it; other prayer groups hear prophecy but they seem more interested in discovering another prophecy than in obeying what has been received. Sometimes one word is enough to carry a whole evening. When God gives you a Word, and you flow with that Word, grace flows, heaven opens, and all kinds of unique spiritual experiences unfold. However, if you have rivalry and contention; everybody anxious to get his own word in, you may have a jumble of words and nothing happening. Paul warns in 1 Corinthians 14, "Let two or three prophets speak at most and the rest weigh their words."[10] Let there be order in the assembly. Let there be building going on!

One thing we learn from reading the Scriptures is

that God does not play games. Sometimes we try to make Him play games. He tells us something once, twice, a third time, and still we do not obey Him. Well, that is playing games with the Lord. We need to figure out what He is saying and obey it. We can not advance; God can not build until we have heard the Word, the first Word, and have obeyed that. God can give us a second Word once we have obeyed the first. If you are wondering why your prayer group is not growing, maybe you have not obeyed what He told you last week, last month, or six months ago. God can not build unless we hear His Word and obey it. Rufus Mosely, a famous evangelist once said, "You know, I never have had a problem with guidance in my life, just with obedience." That is quite a profound statement, and I think one that is very true for most people. I think if all of us want to be honest, we would say that we really do know our duty, but that we have not done it yet. I do not think the problem is guidance. Particularly if you have been in the renewal for a while, the problem ordinarily is not guidance, but rather obedience. We need to come back to that sense of the Hebrew word listen, which means to hear and to obey simultaneously.

The fifth rule for charismatic discernment is to discern as a body, to be a member of a body. There is an injunction: "beware the lone prophet, or beware the lone wise man, or beware the lone wise woman." Thus, it is important that one become part of a body, that he get group discernment. Submit your discernment to leaders of your group. There is safety in the body. Seek the Word of God together. When a group is together as a unity seeking the Word, be the group large or small, what happens is that the same Word is often received by more than one person. When this happens, you know it is the Word of God and you see the body being built. On a larger scale this can be seen at conferences when people from the East and the West come together, and upon comparing journals and logs, find that the Lord is speaking the same kinds of things to all of them, regardless of geographic location. Truly there is one Spirit and He is communicating the same things to all the Christians who are listening to Him. Beware of not being part of a body; beware of not submitting your discernment to elders and to leaders. The failure of obedience has cost many a charismatic his whole life. We need to submit, submit the Word we are hearing to leadership, to others, to the group, to the family.

Families can and should pray together. Even if a husband and wife can not pray at the same hourly time, they can still share with each other the Words received. It can be rather amazing when a husband or wife goes to share a Word received and finds that the same Word was received by the other at a different time or under different prayer circumstances. Beware of doing everything that I am saying without being part of a body, without submitting what you are doing to a body and to direction. The protection of obedience and the protection of the body are needed. Be sure to submit to the guidance of elders, brothers, sisters, spiritual directors and the like.

The sixth and last point of charismatic discernment that I want to stress is that the Word must be pondered. When Simeon told Mary, "a sword will pierce your heart,"[11] she pondered the Word. That is what we need to do as well. Often God will give us a Word which we will hear and not understand or might even find disturbing, but these Words must still be pondered. Elisha the prophet was called by the king "the disturber of Israel." As someone once said, God likes "to comfort the troubled and trouble the comfortable." Sometimes the Words received may be troubling, but ponder them. Do not say that Word is not for me; I do not like that Word; give me another Word. If you have asked for a Word in faith, receive it obediently and ponder it. Let that Word minister to you. In my own personal life some of the Words that I rejected at first ministered eventually much life to me, as I sat with them, pondered them and let them grow within me. Do not let a single Word of God drop to the ground; put your Words into a journal and periodically ponder them. You will not need a retreat master; just your journal, with which you will see how the Spirit has been teaching and guiding you, and you will be able to put it all together, to be able to see patterns emerge over the days, weeks and months. As you ponder the Word, you will be saying, "Wow!" Suddenly clarity will come to your life. Suddenly you will know for sure what God has been saying to you and you will be walking tall.

Along these lines there is another point: If you do not understand a Word that God has given to you, another thing you can do is say, "Lord, I do not understand that Word. Tell me what it means." I guarantee you, not very much time will go by before you get an answer. Maybe the answer will not be given in the way you expected. A conversation with a friend, a second "rayma," a sermon in church, and suddenly you will be aware that God is responding to you. So, if you do not understand a Word, ponder it and then ask God questions; He will give you answers. If you do not ask, God will not respond but if you address your questions to Him you will most assuredly receive answers.

[1] 1 Timothy 5:23
[2] Matthew 23:10
[3] Jeremiah 31:34
[4] John 6:45
[5] Matthew 18:3
[6] I Samuel 3:9
[7] I Corinthians 1:30
[8] I Corinthians 14:4
[9] Proverbs 29:18
[10] 1 Corinthians 14:29
[11] Luke 2:35

CHAPTER 8

Tapping Into Wisdom

Throughout this book I have been trying to share an exciting vision of a tremendous spirit of wisdom, a body of wisdom, that we can tap into just as the people of the 1840's tapped into mountains of gold. There was gold out there and everyone was rushing to it. Today, we should be as excited about seeking wisdom; we should be able to sense that it is there, about to be experienced like the power that has already been experienced in the renewal. Wisdom has hardly begun to be tapped; yet God is saying, "Come and get it."

How do we tap into wisdom? Let me begin my comments by quoting three different books in the Bible — Wisdom, Ephesians and Revelation. Wisdom 1:7, for years, was the entrance antiphon for Pentecost Sunday. "The Spirit of the Lord fills the whole world, is all embracing and knows man's utterance." Ephesians 4 makes a similar statement commenting that Jesus ascended into heaven to give gifts to man and that He would fill the universe.[1] We are now living in the fullness of Christ. He is amongst us. The giant Christ is all over this universe, and His Spirit is always speaking. In the book of Revelation John pleaded with the people, "Listen to what the Spirit is saying."[2] I would like to compare the Holy Spirit to a 24-hour radio station that never stops broadcasting. The exciting thing, my brothers and sisters, is that we can tune into that station anytime we want, and for as long as we want. The Spirit of the Lord is on; He is on the air, and we can tune in to Him. You can tap into the Spirit of God in prayer, and in wisdom-seeking.

An important point to note at this time is the answer to these questions: Who takes the initiative in the process of your receiving wisdom? Who takes the initiative in prayer? I believe that most Christians think they do. "Oh, it is time for me to pray." "I am going to try to get in touch with God. Hey, God!" or, "God, I want some wisdom." It is almost as if we are in the Old Testament. "God, open the heavens and come down." And the Lord of course is replying, "I came down a long time ago. I am here. I am in your heart." Similarly we sometimes pray, "Come Holy Spirit," as if He were not right here in our hearts. Who takes the initiative? If you understand Scripture and theology correctly, man does not; God takes the initiative. All theology, all prayer must be a call-response theology, a call-response prayer. It is God who calls and man who responds.

Louis Evely once stated, "It is not that man calls to God and God does not answer. It is that God calls to man and man does not answer."[3] We think that we are knocking at God's door and the reality is that He is knocking at our door. I would like to explode a kind of myth that is widely accepted as true all around the world today. The myth is that man is constantly searching for God. "I am searching for God; I am searching. Come to this school. Read this book. Take this course. Search for God. Search for the spirit of the universe," and so on. I heard Dennis Bennett talk on this idea of searching, and a comment he made stands out in my mind. He said, "I have read this Bible carefully many times, and I do not find a single example of a sheep ever finding the shepherd!" The whole thing is in the wrong perspective because man does not search for God and find His; God is in search of man. Dennis Bennett's thought was that if we were smart, we would just go "baa, baa!" God will leave the other ninety-nine and go after the one. The person you are most concerned about, God is more concerned about. He has been searching for that person for years. God is out there; you do not have to twist His arms. He wants to pour out His wisdom on us more than we want to receive it. The problem is not getting God to impart His wisdom to us; the problem is opening ourselves up to receive the wisdom that He is pouring out. It is as if there is a glory spout that God has opened in the sky, and that spout is pouring out wisdom, knowledge and power. Like a shower it is open, and all we have to do is enjoy these gifts.

Let me pursue further the analogy between the 24-hour radio station and the Spirit. The Spirit is always communicating; God is always speaking but we do not always hear Him. A hundred years or so ago there were no radios, and it would have been preposterous for mankind to speak about the radio waves that were in the atmosphere. Now, however, everyone is aware of the existence of radios and radio communication, and it is no longer preposterous to speak about radio waves being in the atmosphere. We are aware that radio waves at all times surround us; they even go through our bodies. In order to benefit from these waves that are already in existence, all one needs is a radio receiving set. Depending upon the sophistication of the receiving set being used, a person could tune into a variety of programs, from those aired locally to those that are being broadcast on the other side of the globe. Nothing new needs to be added to our immediate atmosphere to accomplish this; with the radio waves already around us, we could tune into various programs, depending upon the type of radio receiver we used. Let me now transfer the analogy to God. If we can get the right kind of receiving set, we can hear the Spirit all the time. That is much more exciting than listening to radio, AM or FM. When FM came, many people turned off their AM sets; when television came, they turned off their radio sets; when color television came, they turned off their black and white sets. If you are in communication with the Spirit, you will turn off even your color television sets. Why listen to natural, material television when you can have supernatural, spiritual "vision"?

The best of us probably pick up only ten per cent of what God is saying. That is a shame. We are settling for "little" AM transistor radios because we have tuned into God once, because we have heard His voice only once. Do not do that; do not settle for that; open up entirely to the wisdom of the Lord. Learn to tap into wisdom. As with a transistorized radio, you do not have to wait for it to warm up — the program comes right in. Start praying in tongues; start getting into the Spirit and letting the Spirit flow. You will be tuned into the Spirit, and you will be tuned into the rest of the body of Christ everywhere.

Prayer and the turning on of wisdom are the most exciting thing in the world. For most Christians, however, the seeking of wisdom and prayer is a chore because we approach it like work with an "I have to" mentality. "I have to seek wisdom. I have got to work at getting some wisdom." Instead, we should say, "I now have the opportunity to hear God, to receive wisdom. I can let God speak to me." In prayer most of us spend ninety per cent of the time doing all the talking. We do too much talking! Prayer should probably be ninety per cent listening and ten per cent talking.

Teresa of Avila defined prayer as conversation with God, and conversation is a two-way process. If you are smart, when you are in the presence of a greater person, a wiser person, a more beautiful person, you will do most of the listening. Ask the Lord to teach you how to tap into the Spirit. Get to a point where you realize that the initiative is not yours, that wisdom is a gift. Stop trying hard to pray; stop trying hard to get wisdom. Just be in a receptive frame of mind. The God who speaks, the God who thunders in the stillness will communicate with you. Learn to tap into that excitement; all you need is faith and trust. At first, you will just have a one station receiver, then a three-station receiver; gradually you will keep getting better receiving equipment. You should eventually reach the point when you have tremendous receiving equipment; your whole body should be able to hear what God is saying. Revelation 3:20 states, "Behold, I stand at your door and knock. If you hear my knock and open the door, I will come into you and 'sup' with you and I will grant you to sit with me as I have reigned and sat with my father." Sometimes we think, "Lord, I have knocked at your door; I have knocked at your door, and you have not answered." Remember that it is not that man knocks and that God does not answer. God knocks and it is up to man to answer. The initiative is not man's; the initiative is God's.

Once when I was returning from a tremendously rich charismatic conference, I felt that I did not want to leave. It seemed as if the image that Bob Mumford had made reference to was most appropriate. He had made a reference to being under a glory spout, where everything is great, everything is perfect, miracles are happening, joy is abounding, the kingdom is being experienced. It was as if I had been under the glory spout of the Lord, and now I was thinking that I had to go back to my drab world. As I was sitting in the plane, the Lord began to deal with me and my feelings. Our conversation was similar to this:

"Jake, would you like to be under My glory spout always?"

I said, "You mean I can, Lord?!"

He replied, "Yes, I will show you how. My mother will show you how. Go to her, ask her."

One of the things that I heard the Lord saying at that time was that His glory spout had been here ever since Pentecost; the heavens were open; everything was here; we are in the final age; we are in the plenitude of time. His glory had not been cut off; the heavens were not brass anymore; they were open and He had been pouring His life, His Son and His Spirit into the world. The problem was that while the glory was coming down in one place, we had drifted away from it and were saying, "Lord, where are You?" It was as if there were centrifugal forces taking us away from the glory spout — the world, the flesh and the devil. All kinds of centrifugal forces were pulling us this way and pulling us that way.

In the early days of FM I had a radio tuner that taught me a powerful lesson. It had what I called a "drifting dial." I would get beautiful, clear FM music (far surpassing the old AM music) that I was delighted to hear. But after about ten minutes or so the music would begin to get fuzzy, and I would have to go back and adjust the dial in order to bring back the right sound. After the adjustment was made, I would get that crystal clear music once again. However, again, after a while, another adjustment would be needed if I was to continue enjoying the music. The Lord began to show me that I was like that drifting dial. His glory spout was still there; it was I who had drifted away. It was I who needed constant adjusting to stay under the glory spout. He told me that the way to stay under the glory spout was to keep pointing to Jesus. It was like clinging to the Cross. If you wrap your arms around the Cross and cling to it as centrifugal forces pull you this way or pull you that way, you will remain under the glory spout. Satan can attack; the world can be dark, but you will still be under the glory spout. It is just like Paul and Silas. They had their vision. They had their wisdom; they were obeying it even though they were bloodied and beaten and in the stocks. They were still praising God; they were still clinging to the Cross. They did not become a drifting dial; they hung in there praising God. He sent an earthquake that freed them, and that town was evangelized in no time at all.

Paul and Silas stood at the foot of the Cross as Mary did. She always had her eyes on her Lord. She always had her eyes on Jesus. When everyone else left, she was still at the foot of the Cross. That is the secret. The secret of always being under the glory spout is always having your eyes on Jesus. There are going to be times when you are literally going to have to hang on with all you have. You will have to wrap your arms around the Cross and cling to it as to a raft in swirling waters. But then when the clouds go by and you are operating just on radar, not on vision, when the miracle happens, and the power and wisdom come, you will be right there receiving it. You will not be a million miles away.

The other lesson He taught me about staying under the glory spout is: The problem is not only one of clinging to the Cross, but also one of loving. Psalm 37 states, "He will direct your steps in everything." He will give you wisdom. He will show His plan "if you take delight in the Lord." In the New Testament, the statement is made, "Seek first the kingdom of God and everything else will be given to you."[4] Keep your eyes on Jesus. Jesus said, "The law and the prophets can be summed up in the first great commandment: That you love the Lord with your whole heart and your whole soul and your whole mind and your whole strength."

The Lord taught me wisdom in a dynamic and important way through Mary. He said to me, "My mother loved Me with everything she had. I was her son in the flesh; I was her God, so her mind was totally absorbed in Mine. Her mind was never off Me. Her heart was always with Me. All her strength was at My disposal at any moment. She kept the great commandment. You who are called to do the same can love as she did.

"You can receive the gift of love. Love Me as I love you. I think of you all the time; you are always in My heart, and I would use all My strength for you. If you would only return the kind of love I have for you, if you could love Me with your whole heart and your whole mind and your whole strength; if you could be in love with Me, then you would have wisdom." There is wisdom that comes from love. The heart has ears that the mind does not have. When a baby is sick, who is the first one to know that the baby is sick? The baby's mother. The mother senses in the middle of the night that her baby is sick. She senses it with her heart; she hears it with her heart. In a crowd, who hears the voice of the beloved first? The lover hears the voice of the beloved before anyone else knows that he is there. Love hears!

Our problem is not wisdom or the lack of wisdom; our problem is not prayer or the lack of prayer. Our problem is love and the lack of love! Two people who love one another can just sit in silence with each other. Prayer is an expression of love. If we are having difficulty with prayer, it is probably because we do not love. Each of us needs to ask God to forgive us each day for not loving Him as we are commanded to do. We are commanded to be in love with God, to love Him with our whole mind and heart. If we are commanded by Him to do this, it must be possible! He will make it possible for us if we ask Him.

The Holy Spirit is the love in the relationship between the Father and the Son. The Spirit is all love. The Spirit is the love of the Father for the Son and the Son for the Father bouncing back and forth. When we get caught up in the Spirit, when we get caught up in love, we also have the power to love. In the Old Testament they did not have the power to be in love, totally in love, with God. But in the New Testament God sends His Spirit to dwell in our hearts so that we can have the power to be in total love with the Father. We can love Jesus with the very love of the Father. We can love the Father with the very love of Jesus. If we would just yield to more of the Spirit, we would begin to get over our sin of not loving God as we should. If we loved like Mary, we would hear the Father; we could grasp His plan; we would have the mind of Christ. We Christians would have wisdom, and the world could be successfully evangelized.

Thus far in this book I have mentioned different significant points that one should consider in his faith journey towards the acquisition of wisdom. At this time I feel it is important to put these points into summary, into five approaches or plans for tapping into wisdom. First, you have to be aware that wisdom is there. I have already mentioned in detail in Chapter 3 the importance of knowing our wisdom heritage and have given examples like the story about the foolish young man who did not know he was Rockefeller's son and lived as a pauper, and the cheese sandwich story. The first point to be considered as we seek wisdom is that it is of critical importance for each one of us to realize that the fountain of wisdom is there, and that God delights in sharing that wisdom with all His children. We are all a race of prophets, priests and kings; we are all a priestly and royal race. Wisdom is for everyone. I have already extensively discussed the availability of wisdom and have compared the Holy Spirit to the most powerful 24-hour radio station in the world, by way of analogy. The Holy Spirit is on the air all the time, clearly reachable in every city, the "boondocks," the North Pole, everywhere and any-where; His station is always loud, clear and available. Wisdom 1 states that "the Spirit of the Lord fills the whole world." In Ephesians 4, reference is made to the fact that Jesus ascended into heaven "to fill the universe."[5] Thus, we must know that wisdom is readily available; if we do not, if we are unaware of this treasure, we will not be able to realize the gifts of the Spirit before us. We will be like the people who did not know about the Gold Rush and never went West in the 1840's.

The second necessary point to be considered as we seek our wisdom is that the initiative is God's not ours. I think the baptism in the Spirit is largely the transfer from us being lord of our lives, to letting Jesus be Lord of our lives. As I have said, the sheep does not find the shepherd; the shepherd finds the sheep. We do not knock at God's door, He is knocking at our door. He is even washing our feet. Jesus said, "I will make my servants sit down at table and I will serve them."[6] It is God's initiative; it is God who is knocking. We must reply, "I hear you, Lord, come in."

The third point to be considered as we strive to achieve wisdom closely follows the second. It is imperative that we learn to receive, to say with Samuel, "Speak, Lord, your servant listens." This is where faith is so important. We must have faith, expectant faith. There are different levels of faith: intellectual faith, the faith that is assent, the faith that is acceptance, and finally, expectant faith. I have already made reference to the terrible "ninth beatitude" that we, the 20th century people, have added to the gospel: "Blessed are they who expect nothing, for they will not be disappointed." We must have faith, expectant faith; we must be like that woman in the gospel who reached out in her faith and said, "If I just touch Him,"[7] if I ask the Spirit for a "rayma" today, I am sure He will give it to me. "If you ask your father for a fish, will he give you a snake?" "If you ask your father for an egg, will he give you a scorpion?"[8] We should be like little children with expectant faith, and reach out in that faith and say, "Speak, Lord!" For surely if we expect the Lord to come in power, we will not be disappointed.

The fourth point to consider as we learn to tap into wisdom is how important it is that we hang on to the Cross when the testing comes; and it will come; remember Sirach 4 which I described in detail in Chapter 2. Do not just hang in there — hang on! Wisdom 1 says, "if you do not trust Him, you will not receive Him."[9] Sirach 4 states, "but if you fail her (wisdom), she will desert you."[10] If we move away from the glory spout, we will be screaming, "Oh God! Where are You?" I recommend Abbot Geraets beautiful little pamphlet "The Baptism of Suffering," which I mentioned in Chapter 2. We will not always have sunshine; we may be flying with radar, but we can land safely. We will always have the radar of faith coming through the "logos" and the "rayma," the Spirit guiding us. He will be our radar, and He is unfailing.

Finally, the fifth point of importance to be considered as we reach out to accept our gift of wisdom from God is love. Love is the key. The reason so much wisdom is lacking in the church today is that so few love. So few are in love with God. Many of you who are married or who have been in love know what love is. You know what it is to be in love with someone. The person you love is on your mind and in your heart; that loved one's name is magic. You would do anything for that person. You would accept his will, put yourself at his disposal, wash his feet, serve him. That is how God feels toward us. Often, however, we are not aware of that, or we do not believe it. We all know the tragedy of an unrequited love, a one-way love. Remember the old Sacred Heart devotion in the church, "Behold the heart which so loved men and received so little love in return."[11] God is love, and what He thirsts for is our love. Someone asked me to interpret the passage: "Martha, Martha, you are busy about many things, but Mary has chosen the better part, to sit at the feet of Jesus, and it will not be taken away from her."[12] That is truly a wisdom passage!

That is love, to want to sit at the feet of your lover and to want to be instructed by him. Another time I was asked to comment on the Biblical woman at Bethany who went in and broke her precious nard of ointment which was worth 300 gold pieces, and used it on Jesus. A social action extremist might say that the money should have been used for the poor, but Jesus said, "Let her alone, she has done it for me."[13] The aforementioned story is another example of love, giving all you have for another. We must learn the primacy of being in love with Jesus! He has promised to feed His own even in time of famine. The wise man, like the prophet Elisha, will never suffer want because he is under the glory spout and his Father is caring for him. Jesus is shepherding the wise man beautifully and the secret is love.

How do you come into love? How do you come into this kind of love? I think that most of us need to humbly confess that we are not in love with God. That is a good starting point, to be able to say, "Lord, I am not in love with you. Unlike the psalmist I do not dream about you at night." A lot of the psalms turn us off because they are talking about a man in love with God and we are not in love with God. I remember some young people I was once working with who said, "We should throw these psalms out; they are not real." Unfortunately, it was a true statement; the psalms were not real to them because they were not in love with Jesus. When we become in love with Jesus like the psalmist, the psalms will become real.

The best way to love is to pray always. God sent us all that we need to be in love with Him, so that we could carry on our love affair with Him as Jesus did. He sent the Holy Spirit, who is love, who is the very relationship of love between Father and Son. He sent the Holy Spirit into our hearts so we could be a bridal people for Jesus, in order that we could be lovers of God, in order to enable us to spend our time in loving contemplation and praise. We need to pray and ask for the Spirit. Jesus said, "if you ask your Father anything, He will give it to you;"[14] Luke 11 states, "He will give you the Holy Spirit." The way to grow in love is to be in prayer, spend time with God, especially in listening prayer. Jesus enjoins us to "pray always and never cease."[15] To pray always, to pray unceasingly, is really the same thing as to love the Lord with your whole heart. To say the name of Jesus until the name of Jesus was magic, was for generations the way people in the East practiced the injunction to pray always. They breathed in Jesus and breathed out Jesus; they were in love with Jesus; He was at the heart of their life.

With most of us, as with our parents, the way to pray always effectively was probably with the Rosary. Our grandparents and our great-grandparents in Poland, Ireland, Italy, France, Germany, and other countries were constantly praying with beads. Similar to those praying the Jesus prayer, little by little their minds were always on God as Mary's mind was always on God. The genius of the Rosary is, as Mary said, to "think about Jesus all the time as I did." By saying the prayers and fingering the beads of the Rosary, our senses are kept busy. The Rosary removes distractions of our senses and frees our minds to dwell on Jesus, on His mysteries. If

113

you understand them well, the Rosary and the Jesus prayer are exactly the same thing.

Another way of constantly praying is by praying in tongues. In the last analysis praying in tongues is much like the Jesus prayer and the Rosary. When we pray in tongues, we are in the Spirit and we immediately turn on to the Spirit; the Spirit is flowing; we are under the glory spout; we have that 24-hour radio station on that I mentioned earlier, and the reception is good.

There are various other ways of always praying. The breviary, the office of the church and praying seven times a day, all are aids that can be used to enable God's people to become in love with Him and have God always on their minds, the Father always on their minds, Jesus always on their minds.

1 Ephesians 4:10
2 Revelations 2:7
3 Louis Evely, *Teach Us to Pray*
4 Mathew 6:33
5 Ephesians 4:10
6 Luke 12:37
7 Luke 8:44
8 Luke 11:11
9 Wisdom 1:2
10 Sirach 4:19
11 Words of Jesus to Saint Margaret Mary Alocoque
12 Luke 10:40
13 Mark 14:6
14 Luke 11:11
15 Luke 18:1

CHAPTER 9

Mary — Seat of Wisdom

When we pray to Mary as Seat of Wisdom, we do not pray to her as the only seat of wisdom. We pray to her as the seat of wisdom par excellence. But if we understand Marian devotion in the best traditional Catholic way, what it means is to look at Mary and see what we are called to be, to look at Mary and see what the Church is called to be. Chapter 8 of the Vatican Council document on the Church instructs us to look at Mary in this fashion, for we too are called to be seats of wisdom. Mary is not just to be admired as a seat of wisdom, she is to be followed. She does not want admirers; she wants followers; she wants people who will be seats of wisdom as well, hanging on to the Cross of her Son, staying under the glory spout, receiving God's wisdom for the 20th and 21st centuries.

Other beautiful titles that we give Mary besides Seat of Wisdom are Spouse of the Holy Spirit, Daughter of the Father and Mother of Jesus. I am particularly fond of the title Spouse of the Holy Spirit. What that title says to me, what it should say to all of us and to the Church is that we, like Mary, are called to be a spouse, a bride. We are not called to be bridegroom; Jesus is the bridegroom; we are called to be bride. As a bride we should look to Jesus for everything — "His is the kingdom, His is the power, His is the glory." When we and the Church become a spouse of the Holy Spirit, we have that analogized radio station always on. We are tuned in to the Holy Spirit because we want to know what Jesus is doing as He is remaking the face of the earth. When we are a spouse of the Holy Spirit, we will be in love; our mind will be on the Spirit and on His communication. We will be like Mary, the model of bridal union, the model of love, the model of keeping the great commandment. The Church needs Mary as a model in order to learn how to release the power of Jesus and bring about the renewal of the world.

Mary was a charismatic long before the current charismatic renewal existed. A hundred years ago there was not much charismatic life in the Catholic Church, but there was much healing, there was much prophecy. These healings, these prophecies came from Mary; they came from Lourdes; they came from LaSalette; they came from Fatima. Mary was keeping alive the charismatic gifts in the nineteeth and twentieth centuries. Today, in our wise sophistication, which is so very far from wise, we sometimes want to throw Mary out and get on with the "charismatic renewal." Saint Louis DeMontfort made a prophecy some three or four hundred years ago to the effect that God was going to raise up in the Catholic Church an age of Mary which would be followed by an age of the Spirit. He also said that "every time the Holy Spirit

116

finds a Mary heart, He enters there and brings forth Jesus."

If what I am writing is understood properly it would not pose an ecumenical obstacle; rather, it would be an ecumenical help.

Another thing that I can not understand is people with a true Marian devotion today being anti-charismatic. It seems to me that such people could not have a very true Marian devotion. Something is terribly missing if they claim to have a Marian devotion and yet are closed to the Holy Spirit. Of course, some may be justified because they have met the wrong people, just as many people are justified sometimes in not receiving Jesus because they have had the Bible beating them on their head. They were "preached at," instead of being given the opportunity to gently receive the good news of His love.

I remember when I went to the University of Louvain as a young priest, I was surprised at first that in the main hall of the University there was a statue of Mary with a plaque which said that the school was dedicated to Mary, Seat of Wisdom. I had to meditate on that dedication. They had had some learned saints go through that university and yet they had dedicated it to someone who never went to high school or college. During my meditation the words of Jesus came to me: "Father, I give you thanks that you have hidden these things from the wise and revealed them to little ones."[1] Wisdom is for the little. Wisdom is for the lover. Wisdom is for the child. Wisdom is for the person of faith. And Mary is all of the aforementioned and more. Those who have not prayed to Mary yet may need to say a little prayer of repentance. She has been a beautiful mother and wants to continue to be our mother. We need to go to her as a model, as a mother, as an intercessor. Remember the power of her intercession at Cana. Jesus was not about to work a miracle; He said, "My hour has not yet come."[2] Mary's reply was simply, "Do whatever He tells you." Some people say that they do not believe in the intercession of the saints and the intercession of Mary. They should read the account of the wedding at Cana in John 2.

A beautiful prayer to pray is that the Holy Spirit form in you a Mary heart and to pray and ask Jesus to have you appropriate His heart for His mother.

[1] Matthew 11:25
[2] John 2:4

CHAPTER 10

Wisdom — "The Book"

Israel came to realize in its history that wisdom was in the Book, that wisdom was "the Book." The prophet Amos tried to tell the people of the northern kingdom of Israel that their kingdom was about to fall because they were going their own way rather than the way God had revealed to them. He said, disaster is going to strike you. You are going to be conquered by Assyia; this is about to happen.[1] Amos' words are true for today as well. Amos told the people that God said, I tried to bring you back to me by famine and you did not listen. I tried to bring you back by withholding the rain and you did not listen.[2] Just as in our days He tries to bring us back by shortages and plagues, but we do not listen. Amos 8:11 states,

> "Days are coming, says the Lord, when I will send famine upon the land. Not a famine of bread or thirst for water, but for hearing the word of the Lord. And then they shall wander from sea and rove from the North to the East in search of the Lord, but they shall not find it. And when the famine of the word occurs, Israel will be no more."

If disaster is striking our world today, it is because the Christian world is operating now under a famine of the Word, both "logos" and "rayma." Because of the famine of the Word, we will have other famines. When there is a famine of the Word, and a famine of hearing God, all other famines follow; that is what Amos was saying.

The words of Jeremiah also seem to speak to us to-day. The world of Jeremiah was not really able to hear what he was saying; therefore, the Lord told him to write the words down. Have your secretary Baruch write down the prophecies in much the same way the Rome prophecies and the Kansas City prophecies were written down.

> "Then they asked Baruch: 'Tell us, please, how you came to write down all these words.' 'Jeremiah dictated all these words to me,' Baruch answered them, 'and I wrote them down with ink in the book.' At this the princes said to Baruch, 'Go into hiding, you and Jeremiah; let no one know where you are.'
>
> "Leaving the scroll in safekeeping in the room of Elishama the scribe, they entered the room where the king was. When they told him every-thing that had happened, he sent Jehudi to fetch the scroll. Jehudi brought it from the room of Elishama the scribe, and read it to the king and to all the princes who were in attendance on the king. Now the king was sitting in his winter house, since it was the ninth month, and fire was burning in a brazier before him. Each time Jehudi finished reading three or four columns, the king would cut off the piece with a scribe's knife and cast it into the fire in the brazier, until the entire roll was consumed in the fire. Hearing all these

words did not frighten the king and his ministers or cause them to rend their garments. And though Elnathan, Delaiah and Gemariah urged the king not to burn the scroll, he would not listen to them, but commanded Jerahmeel, a royal prince, and Seraiah, son of Azriel, and Shelemiah, son of Abdeel, to arrest Baruch, the secretary, and the prophet Jeremiah. But the Lord kept them concealed.

"This word of the Lord came to Jeremiah, after the king burned the scroll with the text Jeremiah had dictated to Baruch: Take another scroll, and write on it everything that the first scroll contained, which Jehoiakim, king of Judah, burned up. And against Jehoiakim, king of Judah, say this: Thus says the Lord: You burned that scroll, saying, 'Why did you write on it: Babylon's king shall surely come and lay waste this land and empty it of man and beast?' The Lord now says of Jehoiakim, king of Judah: No descendant of his shall succeed to David's throne; his corpse shall be cast out, exposed to the heat of day, to the cold of night. I will punish him and his descendants and his ministers for their wickedness; against them and the citizens of Jerusalem and the men of Judah I will fulfill all the threats of evil which went unheeded.

"Jeremiah took another scroll, and gave it to his secretary, Baruch, son of Neriah; he wrote on it at Jeremiah's dictation all the words contained in the book which Jehoiakim, king of Judah, had burned in the fire, and many others of the same kind in addition."[3]

They eventually found the scroll that Baruch wrote and all that had been spoken in it came true. I think we are having a big crisis in the Church today because we too are having a famine of the Word. We are picking and choosing God's Words. We get a pair of scissors and we cut this Word and then we cut that Word and then exclaim, "Ah! Here is a Word I like." If something does not please us, we throw it away; we throw it over our shoulder into the fire. However, we can not let a Word of God drop to the ground without peril to ourselves and to our world. Isaiah 55 states, "My word comes down from heaven like the rain and snow that soak the earth. It never returns to me void, but accomplishes the purpose for which I sent it."[4] The Word of God is dynamic; it has life; it accomplishes its purpose. If we turn away from the Word, we do so at our own peril. I heard Ralph Martin speaking one time on the main reasons for today's crisis in the church. He felt that the crisis was a result of certain works of Biblical criticism in the 19th century which simply dispensed with the Word of God as a criterion for moral standards and for our life. The discarding of God's Words is what the prophet Amos screamed about; it was what Jeremiah screamed about.

Israel was in exile over 200 years and as the Israelites were coming home to Jerusalem, God raised up the prophet Ezra; He gathered all the lost Words and put them into a book. Ezra helped form the Book; he gathered all the Words he could find and he put together the Scroll. Later he and schools of scribes held the people to this Book so they would not have to go into exile again. Ezra's words basically were, "stick to the book and you will live." The people of Israel were back; Ezra had put all the Words he had found together and was to present this material to the people. Nehemiah describes the scene with the people of Israel attentively listening to the Word:

> "Standing at one end of the open place that was before the Water Gate, he read out of the book from daybreak till midday, in the presence of the men, the women, and those children old enough to understand; and all the people listened attentively to the book of the law. Ezra the scribe stood on a wooden platform that had been made for the occasion; . . . Ezra opened the scroll so that all the people might see it; and as he opened it, all the people rose. Ezra blessed the Lord, the great God, and all the people, their hands raised high, answered, 'Amen, amen!' Then they bowed down and prostrated themselves before the Lord, their faces to the ground . . . Ezra read plainly from the book of the law of God, interpreting so that all could understand what was read. Then Nehemiah, that is His Excellency, and Ezra the priest-scribe and the Levites who were instructing the people said to all the people: 'Today is holy to the Lord your God. Do not be sad, and do not weep' — for all the people were weeping as they heard the words of the law. He said further: 'Go, eat rich foods and drink sweet drinks, and allot portions to those who had nothing prepared; for today is holy to our Lord. Do not be saddened this day, for rejoicing in the Lord must be your strength!' "[5]

They celebrated with great joy because they were back in their land and they had the Word of God, their Book, and they pledged themselves to keep to what the Book said. That was wisdom. The people of Israel pledged to use the Book as a textbook, to learn from and live by the Book. The Bible is a school; it is a library. Ezra restored this school to Israel. He told the people to learn the Book; of course, it did not have all the Books we now have, but he put together what the Lord made available to him. "The beginning of wisdom is to get wisdom," and we do that by love and by the Word. Today we need an Ezra who will gather the Word, interpret the Word, make the library of the Word available to the people so that we will not perish, so that we will not have a famine. If we do not have a famine of the Word, if we do not have a famine of the "logos" and the "rayma," we will have prosperity. If the "logos" and the "rayma" are flowing, prosperity will flow; however, if the "logos" and the "rayma" are not flowing, famine will come. God will have no other choice.

A quick survey of the books of the Bible reveals that numerous topics are covered within the Word. There are chapters on how to bring your children up, how to relate as husbands, how to relate as wives; there are enormous amounts of practical wisdom throughout the Bible. For example, today in the renewal there is much talk about the need for seeking medical advice; Sirach 38 speaks about the relationship between faith and medicine and can shed much light on many of the questions about seeking medical advice. I recommend a book like Ralph Martin's book, *Husbands, Wives, Parents, and Children,* which is basically the wisdom combed from the Bible on family life. On the same subject I also recommend Larry Christenson's book entitled, *The Christian Family.* The Bible is a total library.

I am often reminded of the parable Jesus related

about the unjust steward. The unjust steward was fired for being a crook, but he was a smart man. Before he had to leave, he did a few things. He went to some of his master's creditors and said, "How much do you owe my master?" The answers varied, "A hundred barrels of wheat. Eighty barrels of oil." The unjust steward told his master's creditors to change the amounts they owed to lower figures. The steward hoped that people whom he helped would welcome him into their homes once his master had fired him. When the master learned of the actions of the unjust steward, he commended him for his enterprise, his prudence, his wisdom. Jesus sarcastically said, "Alas, the children of this generation are wiser than the children of the light."[6] What He was saying to us was "How dumb you people are. The criminals, the Mafia, the Communists are smarter than you are. If only you would get some wisdom, if only you would get smart. You should be running the world within My power and wisdom. You are sitting back like the last place team in the American league when you should be in first place."

Let me give you an example of how dumb we are. Most prayer groups throughout the country have a Life in the Spirit Seminar. We have a whole system of beautiful Spirit-filled Life in the Spirit Seminars being given across the country. People are receiving the Spirit; they are being turned around; new lives are surfacing. Many prayer groups have added a Christian Foundations course to their Life in the Spirit Seminars. But usually that is the end of formal training in most prayer groups. We received the information for both the Life in the Spirit Seminar and the Foundations courses from the Word of God Community in Ann Arbor. The Word of God Community, however, did not stop at the Foundations course level as most of the other prayer groups have. I remember in the early days, receiving the information from Ann Arbor before the manual was printed. I used to get tapes, listen to the tapes of the sessions, and then teach the material presented in the tapes to the groups in Providence. (Getting one of the hundreds of teaching tapes that now exist, digesting it, and giving it to your people is still a very valid way of disseminating information today. To do this is so simple that anyone living in the North Pole could teach all the Eskimos around him the latest teaching in the renewal without ever leaving his home village.)

The point I am making is simply that there is no excuse for not having wisdom and good teaching today.

If we choose to stay in the first grade, we will not become very free in life. The Life in the Spirit Seminar is kindergarten; Foundations is the first grade. The Word of God at Ann Arbor added to Foundations — grades 2, 3, 4, 5, 6, 7, 8, high school and college. Much of the rest of the renewal is still back in the first grade saying, "I am wise." We have what we call in the renewal "the revolving door syndrome." The average life of a charismatic in a prayer group is about two years. The reason for this revolving door syndrome is that the people go to kindergarten, they go to first grade, they stick around for awhile; there is nothing else, so they leave. There is no more teaching, no wisdom, no Ezras. There are tremendous amounts of teaching available, but sadly we have not learned how to market the material properly. Great books, great tapes are gathering dust on shelves and are not being sold; magazines such as "New Covenant" and "Pastoral Renewal" have not the circulation they should have. The wisdom is available to us; all we need do is to reach out and grasp it.

[1] Amos 1, 2; 2:4 et.al
[2] Amos 4:6-11
[3] Jeremiah 36:17-32
[4] Isaiah 55:10
[5] Nehemiah 8:3
[6] Luke 16:8

CHAPTER 11

Wisdom After Pentecost

We are living at a time which in many ways is more advantageous to us than Biblical times. We are more blessed than John the Baptist, Jesus said. Because we are living after Pentecost, the least person in the kingdom is greater than he. We are living in the fullness of time; we are living in the last age; we are living in the plentitude. The Spirit of the Lord now fills the universe and is available to everybody. Today wisdom is prophetic; wisdom is not only "logos," but it is also "rayma." Jesus promised that the Holy Spirit would come to teach us everything and guide us into all truth. We are in that time now; we are living in a prophetic age after Pentecost. Imagine what could happen if the Evangelicals and the Pentecostals joined together with the "logos" and the "rayma." Imagine what such an ecumenical movement could produce for the world! God is trying to tell us that such a unity can be made, that the age in which we are living is a most powerful one. Jesus' message is, "Father, I pray that they may be one as we are one so that the world might come to know that you sent me, and that you love them as you have loved me."[1]

There seem to be many "thorny" questions today; however, through the guidance of the Spirit, the solutions are available to us. The Spirit knows how to put everybody in the body in a different place. He knows who should be an eye and an ear and a finger and a thumb and the like. If we ask Him, He will inform us.

One question that seems to be a controversial one today deals with parish renewal. My training in the seminary taught me that parish renewal was something that proceeded through the regular channels of the Pope, the Bishop, the pastor, and finally, the parish. My training, coupled with the experience I had had at Saint Patrick's, made my statements on parish renewal very firm. In Providence we had successes in our efforts of parish renewal following the traditional methods. The pastor and I were together; we were in the renewal and the parish was being renewed. Based on the success at Saint Patrick's, we thought it could and should happen like that all over the country, all over the world. We found out differently when we started going to conferences and talking to others. We found out that our parish was unique. At conference after conference I was challenged with questions like, "Where else is parish renewal happening in the way you describe?" In our case God had put together the magic ingredients, pastor on fire, filled with the Spirit, a big body already in the renewal and a parish in need of new life; things seemed to come together and the parish was renewed. We thought it could happen like that everywhere; we were leading the renewal in our area along those lines; everything had to be the way we had experienced it. The Lord had to take me by the hair of the head and show me that that was not entirely wisdom for everybody. It was for us, but we should not export it to everybody.

I began to learn the hard way from history, which is always so instructive, that parish renewal and the syndrome I was in was not even the ordinary way renewal happened. What we had experienced was the exceptional way. Renewal had rarely, if ever, come to the Church through parish renewal. In fact, putting renewal prematurely in the parish had often killed renewal efforts. I recommend a very beautiful wisdom book, *Unordained Elders and Renewal Communities,* by Steve Clark; this book shows that throughout history successful renewal came from "new wine in new skins." I think this book is one of the most important in the renewal today. It has opened my eyes and made me take a 180 degree turn from what I had previously thought about renewal. If Francis put all his men at the service of a pastor in a particular parish in Umbria, we might never have had the Franciscan renewal of the 13th century; and yet, parish renewal happened through Francis. What church in Christendom does not have the Stations of the Cross or a Christmas crib, and both the stations and the crib come from Francis. Francis' renewal overflowed like a fountain and influenced all parishes. But if you "put new wine into old skins" prematurely, both get hurt. We may come on too strong with people not in the renewal and say, "You have to be in the renewal!" We destroy them; they may be doing fine with their old wine skins, and the Lord may be saying, "Leave them alone." The Lord may be saying to us as He did to Francis or

Ignatius or any religious founder, "Just put new wine in new skins." I believe that this age needs a new experience, a new and fresh experience. It should be brought about in the Church, in loyalty to the Church, under the Bishop, under the Pope. The secret of religious success down through the centuries has always been loyalty to the Church. We must have obedience and loyalty to the Church. But that does not necessarily mean you are going to go and consult your pastor who might be anti-renewal, or indifferent to it. I have given the advice; many have given the advice, "Go and lay down your lives in your parish, die in your parish for parish renewal." That was not always wisdom! That was often Galatians 3, "Oh, you foolish Galatians going back into law, putting yourself in places where the gifts of the Spirit can not even operate, extinguishing the Spirit. Oh, you foolish Galatians, did you start by law or the Spirit? Why are you quenching what God is doing?" Tom Twitchell writes in his book, *That They All Might Be One,* that many of us have heard the advice to go and lay down your lives and die in your parish for its renewal, and we followed it. We went back to our parishes, we laid down our lives and we died, and everything else died.

I am not writing against parish renewal; I am for parish renewal. Communities like The Word of God at Ann Arbor and The People of Praise at South Bend have often been accused of being dangerously on the point of schism, not very Catholic and not very interested in parish renewal. Much of that controversy has been very harmful and personally I think that history will show that these people, these com-

131

munities, have done far more for parish renewal than any of us are presently aware.

There are two equally valid ways of living in the Catholic Church. No one is a second class citizen. There is the way of living in the Catholic Church as a member of a parish and there is the way of living in the Catholic Church as a member of a religious order, a third order or a secular institute. Both are equally acceptable, and both have equal right of citizenship in the Church. There has always been a tension between the diocesan structures and religious orders. There has always been a tension between Peter and Paul; Paul had to tell Peter off. In Galatians 2, Paul had to stand up to Peter. That is being Catholic; that is in our tradition; that tension is healthy. There is more than one valid way of relating in the Church today. You can relate either in the tradition of a parish or of a religious order. Parish renewal will come; it has to come. If there were no parishes today, in ten years we would have to create them. But do not be the rabbit that gets ahead of the tortoise; do it God's way. Do it with wisdom. Maybe right now God is calling you into the kind of new wine and new skin tradition, loyal to the Church, but not yet in a parish structure, like Francis.

I want to write a word in defense of covenant communities. Many people, including me, and I repent of it, often thought that perhaps covenant communities were a very dangerous trend. The Lord has taken me and turned me around 180 degrees on this, so I can write about it. I refrained from going to Ann Arbor for a long time and turned in other directions for help. The men of Ann Arbor were always men of the

Church; they were in contact with their Bishop, their pastors. In the beginning they wanted to do it the parish way, but God never allowed that to happen. Finally, they have been so beautifully vindicated. A new thing has happened in the Church. From Rome's suggestion and the work of Cardinal Suenens and Bishop Povish of Lansing, they have established a new fellowship in The Word of God Community.

They have established an official Roman Catholic fellowship inside the ecumenically approved Word of God Community. At the same time, they have approved three other ecumenical fellowships, a Lutheran fellowship, an Episcopal fellowship and a Free Church fellowship. Everyone in the Word of God Community, those 2000 or so beautifully covenanted ecumenical people, although they are community members, are also truly ecumenical; they have strong ties with their own church. Their own church is being aided and stengthened; parish renewal will be aided and reinforced by this process, which is all under the direction of all the churches; none of the churches are hurt. This renewal is all coming from the grass roots and it is approved from on top. It is a beautiful example as well as a stamp of approval by the Roman Catholic Church of what many of us called dangerous. Perhaps, we need to go to learn about wisdom in places like Ann Arbor. Jesus said, "You must be wise as serpents and simple as doves."[2] That statement might apply to a large extent in parish renewal. There are all kinds of covenant communities. There is not just one model. Do not put them all in one box. Let the Spirit grow tulips, roses, violets and everything He wants to grow. Look to the various models, but be open to what the Spirit may lead you to do.

There is a problem in the renewal today of law coming back to quench the Spirit. The worst kind of law is charismatic law because you think you are free; you think you are in the Spirit. For example, the person who sings in tongues at the least provocation, the same tone, the same pitch, the same song all the time — that is law. When singing in tongues occurs and it is from the Spirit, you can almost see the Spirit conducting saying, "soft, soft, loud, loud, crescendo, crescendo, weeping, moaning, laughing, soft, jubilant." If the prayer group always has the same volume, the same tune, the same length of time, that is not Spirit; that is law. Or, the prayer meeting that automatically starts with tongues every week, following the same formula right through it, so much so that you can always predict what is going to happen next; that is law. The Spirit must lead; He might tell you one night to have a witness all night; another night you might be told to have a teaching. The most important thing is to be open to the Spirit.

Beware of charismatic law; it is the worst kind of law. The Pentecostal Churches had a difficult time accepting the fact that the Spirit could speak in the Catholic Church. Many individual Pentecostals from David Duplessis on down were ostracized for being so open to Catholic charismatics and Episcopal charismatics. This type of rigidity, of bias is an example of charismatic law. The Galatians started in the Spirit and then went back to law; many people today have started in the Spirit: beautiful prayer meetings, full of the Spirit, and then they have been put back into parish renewal prematurely and their fire was extinguished. That is "Galatianism." If the Spirit tells you to do that, if the Spirit clearly lets you know, "that is what I want you to do: go back there, stay there, die, lay down your life;" then you must go back. If you hear the Spirit telling you to go back, you must, even if you see no fruit, even if you are to die. But do not do it unless the Spirit tells you to do so!

Another example of charismatic law is in the sermons, in the preaching, in the teaching. We have a series and we are going to go right through the series, A, B, C, D, E, F, G, H, I, J. Or, it is Christmas time and one goes to the file and takes out last year's Christmas sermon. He was very inspired last Christmas; therefore, the sermon is given again. Or, last year at this time I was in Oshkosh and this year I am in New York; therefore, I can give the same teaching I have given before. These are all examples of law. God will give us a fresh word for a fresh audience every year, every day. Pray before you preach; pray before you teach, and give to others what the Spirit gives to you. In our radio ministry in Providence, many people ask us, "What do you teach? Do you go through the Bible?" We quickly answer, "No!" We have a ministry of prayer and it seeks the Lord and asks the Spirit, "What do you want us to teach this week?" Whatever the Spirit tells us as a body is what we teach; we teach the "logos" and the "rayma."

Another example of law can be found in the teaching of some social actionists. They feel frustrated when their teaching and preaching seem to fail. But it fails because it is based on the law, not on the Spirit. I speak from personal experience in this case. Many priests, myself and friends included, have gone up into the pulpit and preached the beatitudes. "You must feed the hungry; you must get out into the inner city — blessed are the peacemakers." We have placed guilt on many listeners by asking what is the matter with them, by telling them they are Christians and must get out and do what the gospel states. Matthew 25, "I was hungry and you gave me to eat."[3] This is Christianity, we say. We have exhorted the people to get out there and we have become angry when they did not go. We suffered frustrations and many left the priesthood because of these frustrations. Well, the problem was not always with the people; often the problem was with us. The Christians were not moving because they were not yet ready. They could not follow the beatitudes as yet because many had not yet met Jesus; many still needed to be evangelized. Pope Paul VI was aware of this; he said, "We must begin evangelizing the world, and we must begin with Christians."[4] Most of our people need evangelizing. We were evangelized when we came into the renewal; most people are not ready to hear the beatitudes until they have met Jesus, until they love Him and know that He loves them.

These examples all point to the importance of praying before you teach or preach. If you are going to come into a congregation and give them a teaching, beware of giving them one that you like. Sometimes a thought comes to mind and we quickly, without confirmation, assume that the thought is a "rayma." I am always wary when I hear someone say, "This word comes to my mind." Sometimes it is from the Spirit, but it still needs to be tested. Only the Spirit knows at what point that congregation is. The Spirit may say, "Look, this group is at point 'H,' and what I want you to do is take them from 'H' to 'I.'" The only place you will be effectively able to lead them is from H to I. If they are at M, the only way you can effectively teach them is to take them from M to N. You will be ineffective if you attempt to take them from M to Q. You must seek the Spirit, pray to Him; He will tell you whether the people are at point H or whether they are at point M or whether they are at point A. Once the Spirit has told you where the people are, He will inform you how you should proceed so that the group may go to point I, or N or B or even say how to evangelize them.

I am a pastor and it would be impossible for me to know all the people in my congregation and the exact point at which each person is in his walk with the Lord. The Spirit, however, knows all things; therefore, He can easily tell me how to proceed. My ministry and I spend time in prayer, seeking the Lord, asking the Lord, "Lord, what do the people need? At what point are they?" He always tells us so very beautifully. I preach the word He gives and the people get moved from H to I, B to C and the like. It does not make any difference to God whether the people are at point B or point X. The only thing He is interested in is giving them the opportunity to move from B to C or X to Y.

There appear to be many neat answers around today; beware of some of them. For example, some in the Church today operate under the principle of meeting needs. Beware of this principle! There are so many needs in a congregation that no one human being could begin to meet all the needs! Only God can meet the needs of a congregation. There is some good advice in this regard in both the book of Proverbs and the book of Psalms. Proverbs 19:2 states, "Without knowledge even zeal is not good; and he who acts hastily blunders;" the thought is continued in verse 21, "Many are the plans in a man's heart, but it is the decision of the Lord that endures." With wisdom we will not be overworked. The psalms confirm the idea that only what the Lord desires done will be truly successful. Psalm 127 states, "If God builds the city it gets built. If God watches a city it gets watched. It is vain for you to get up early in the morning and work till late at night. God gives to His beloved in sleep." God is a good boss; He only has you working an eight-hour day. He gives you eight hours sleep. If this is not happening something is wrong. Our God is a God of rest and sabbaths, of peace and joy. Chances are, if you are overworked and overwrought, you are out of wisdom. If God calls you to do a certain thing, you will find He is very reasonable. He will give you all you need to complete the project He calls you to. Much true wisdom is lost through the use of so-called human wisdom.

There is a newspaper that has as a part of its heading this quotation: "The Truth Will Make You Free." The truth will not make you free. The Bible does not say, "The truth will make you free;" that is taking a part of the whole and falsifying it. John 8:31 states, "If you remain in my word, you will become my disciple; then you will know the truth and the truth will make you free." The above passage is not saying to go out into the world and learn the truth about things because the truth will make you free; rather it is saying, become a disciple of Jesus Christ and the words of Jesus will make you free. I believe that if the newspaper editors quoting that line realized the error of its wording, that the words would be removed from its heading.

Another misconception is the idea that everybody is going to heaven, that you can do whatever you want and it will work out in the end. I do not believe that is so. Anyone who does believe that to be so should read Sirach 16, where God says, "Great as His mercy is His punishment; He judges men each according to his deeds."[5] That may be a hard word. It may not gel with everyone, but it is the Word of God. Another point where we lose wisdom is in the misconception that God hears all prayers. The Bible does not say that God hears all prayers. The Bible says that God hears all the prayers of those who fear Him. There is a distinction between the just, wise man, and the unjust, unwise man. You can not do whatever you want and then pray to God and expect Him to rescue you. He may sometimes; He is a God of mercy, but what the Bible says is that God hears the prayers of His children. "Abba" hears the prayer of His sons and His daughters! The Bible goes on to say that the heavens are closed to the prayers of the unjust. God also states, "Because I called to you and you did not answer, when you call to Me, I will not answer."[6] Thus, prayer is not automatic; we need wisdom, we need to ask the Spirit how we should proceed.

[1] John 17:20
[2] Matthew 10:16
[3] Matthew 25:31-46
[4] Exhortation "Evangelii Nuntiandi" — 1975
[5] Sirach 16:12
[6] Isaiah 65: 12

CHAPTER 12

The Message of the Spirit to the Church Today

At this point I want to write a little like a "wisdom prophet." In Jesus everything comes together. Jesus is the king, the priest, the prophet and the wise man; and we are all the body of Christ. Therefore, today wisdom is prophetic and the prophet is wise. We are luckier than the prophets of the Old Testament; whereas the Spirit came upon them only occasionally, we are able to tap into the Spirit, to turn on that analogized 24-hour station. We are living in the fullness of the kingdom; Jesus has come and opened the gates; the flood gates are open and we are living in the plentitude. Wisdom today is prophetic wisdom. In the book of Revelation, John continually makes this statement: "Listen to what the Spirit is saying to the churches."[1] At the end of every one of the letters is the statement, "He who has ears to hear, let him hear."[2] I think that there are many things that the Spirit is saying to the Churches. The Spirit is speaking through Pope John Paul II; He spoke through Pope Paul VI; He is speaking through the leadership of our Church. I am going to limit myself, however, to comments on what the Spirit is saying to the renewal. I

141

recognize that the Spirit is speaking in many avenues, but wish to write my comments on only one area — that being the Words heard in the renewal. I want to home in on two particular areas: The first, the Rome prophecies and the second, the Kansas City prophecies.

If you did not believe the Rome prophecies, and many in the renewal never did, you can read them now in your daily newspapers, or watch them on your local television news broadcasts. Not long ago members of my ministry and I were watching and listening to the television presentation of the news. After the program was over, I commented "The news can certainly be depressing." One of my companions quickly responded, "It is fifty times worse than the Rome prophecies were in 1975." That certainly seemed to be a true statement. The Rome prophecies were not depressing; they were very hope-filled. When God prophesies, He never condemns and leaves you down; He always picks you up and gives you hope. He started those prophecies, which incidentally came from the altar of Saint Peter's, by saying, "My people, because I love you, I am telling you what is going to happen in the next few years." If you had heard Him then and could take a loving daddy telling you to buckle your seat belts and get ready for the times ahead, you would be in pretty good shape today. But if you said, like the king in Jeremiah, let us cut that Word up and throw it away; let us cut this Word up and throw it away, you may not be ready.

You may not be ready today for the tragedy that is coming upon the world. If your groups have not heard those Words, I urge you to go back to them. They are part of what the Spirit is saying to the Church today. They are not optional. I believe the same message is being given throughout Christendom in every Church, Catholic, Protestant and Pentecostal. The Spirit is saying, buckle your seat belts, hard times are coming, "I am taking Israel out to the desert to allure her once again to my heart, to espouse her once again." You are going to have to go out to the desert and rediscover the Word again.

We must listen to the prophetic Word that has come forth from Rome and to subsequent prophecies well attested to in the renewal. They are not optional. Sometimes in the renewal people say, "Well, I follow this trend of renewal, and I follow that trend of renewal. I follow parish renewal trends. I follow covenant renewal trends." Some of the divisions in the renewal come from people who have heard the Word and followed it; others come from people who have heard the Word and have not followed it — that is not a legitimate division! This is a hard word, but it needs to be stated. Many of the trends are not legitimate because they are formed by people in disobedience, people who have heard the Word and have not followed it.

Listen to what the Spirit is saying to the Church today! Judgment is coming upon the household of God. God is saying, "Look, I am bringing an end to an era." I do not believe that God is saying, "I am bringing the world to an end. The rapture is coming tomorrow." I think that is a fundamentalist view. The Rome prophecies did not say that. The Rome prophecies said, "I am preparing an age of glory; I am going to make my people one; I am going to bring about an era of evangelization such as the world has never seen before." Buckle your seat belts; what God is saying is, "I am calling an end to the era of man. I am going to introduce an era of Jesus again, an era of the Word again."

Man is not the measure of all things; the "enlightenment" is going to be by-passed and seen as dark. Christ, the measure of all things, is going to prevail again. That is what it means when we say and sing, "Jesus is coming; Come, Lord Jesus." He is going to come on the clouds with power and majesty. He will kick up a few clouds, darken the sun and the moon; this is apocalyptic imagery for the coming of Jesus. God loves His world so much; God loves His people so much that He is stepping in in a special way. Jesus is going to come and intervene; He is doing it now; judgment is already happening. God has already begun His judgment with the household of God; He is tearing down what should not exist so that He can build. Cities will be repeopled; as Isaiah says, "I am going to restore the ruined homesteads."[3] Jesus is going to come and make it safe for old people to walk in the city streets again, for the young people to play in the streets again. Jesus is going to come and be Lord; our churches will be open again. But in the meantime, as it says in Amos I, "The Lion roars;" the axe is at the root of the tree.

The other Word that has not been heard is the Kansas City prophecy, "Mourn and weep, mourn and lament, for the body of My Son is broken." Have you mourned or wept yet; has your prayer group mourned or wept yet? If not, we need to repent. "Mourn and weep, for the body of My Son is broken," is a well-attested-to Word of the Lord. We are called to evangelize the world by Pope Paul VI's "Evangelii Nuntiandi;" but we can not evangelize the world, as John 17 says, until we are one. "Father, I pray that the Christians may be one." May they be in us with all the power of God flowing through the body as it flowed through Jesus. "May they be in us so that the world can get evangelized."[4] If all the power of all the streams of Christianity came together, if the body of Christ were one instead of 55, then the Christians would be able to proclaim Jesus to the world. If we could come together and be that one body of Jesus, loving one another with the power of God flowing through us, all the nations would come to the mountain of Zion and the world would get evangelized and know the love of the Father.

We need the wisdom of Israel, wisdom that is practical, wisdom that hears and obeys. We need obedience; we do not need options. I think we need some generals in the renewal, some apostles. I believe we need to pray that apostles be raised up, generals, architects like Paul who know how to put it all together. The renewal is dispersed into a million fragments. We are at a time similar to what happened with Ezra and Nehemiah ten years after the return from exile when Israel was a shambles again. God raised up prophets like Haggai and Zechariah, leaders like Ezra and Nehemiah; they gathered the Book to move the people again. God has said, "Here you are living in your own paneled homes; you have all been baptized in the Holy Spirit, and My renewal is going to pieces. What about My house?" After ten years the people of Israel needed renewing, and I think today the charismatic renewal needs renewing. It needs renewing by wisdom. There are wise men around today; we must look to them, listen to them. Pray to Mary, Seat of Wisdom, that we may listen to and obey the Spirit so that we may once again become one, and so that the world may know the love God has for His people.

[1] Revelation 2:7 et. al.
[2] Ibid.
[3] Isaiah 61:4
[4] John 17:20, paraphrased.

THE POST CHARISMATIC EXPERIENCE
The New Wave of the Spirit   4.50

Rev. Robert A. Wild. "Is the Charismatic Renewal dying?" "Where is the Movement headed?" These burning questions are proposed in depth for all who are actively involved in the Charismatic Renewal and who question the exodus of many former members. They will find this expert appraisal encouraging and challenging. All who have ever been touched by the Spirit in the Charismatic Movement will discover herein fresh insight and prophetic challenge in their developing life in the Spirit. This book is also for those who feel they have "passed through" the Charismatic Renewal, who no longer openly practice the Gifts of the Spirit and feel vaguely disquiet about it. Fr. Wild is a resident of Madonna House in Combermere, Ontario, and is the author of the popular *Enthusiasm in the Spirit* (Ave Maria Press).   ISBN: 0-914544-50-0

THIRSTING FOR GOD IN SCRIPTURE   2.95

James McCaffrey, O.C.D. This book is an important aid to a deeper understanding of the Bible as a means of slaking our thirst for God and of drawing closer to Him. The reader is guided through several texts of Scripture at length and given copious references which enable him/her to compare and contrast the ways of the Spirit. All those thirsting for truth will profit from Fr. McCaffrey's guidance as they prayerfully approach Scripture with him.   ISBN: 0-914544-55-1

THE ANGEL'S QUEST   6.95

Kathy Thomas. This is a rarity in children's fiction: a book that radiates inspiration and love and at the same time is an engrossing story. Newly orphaned Baby Thoma is taken by his guarding angel on a search for a new home. This well-paced tale, profusely and charmingly illustrated, brings magic and wonder to readers and listeners alike. Illustrated by Jacqueline Seitz. Aged 3-7, hard cover, 2-color 10" × 7".   ISBN: 0-914544-99-3

SPIRITUAL DIRECTION
Contemporary Readings   5.95

Edited by Kevin Culligan, O.C.D. The revitalized ministry
of spiritual direction is one of the surest signs of renewal in today's Church. In this book seventeen leading
writers and spiritual directors discuss history, meaning,
demands and practice of this ministry. Readers of the
book should include not just a spiritual elite, but the en-
tire Church — men and women, clergy and laity, members of religious communities.   ISBN: 0-914544-43-8

PRAYER:
The Eastern Tradition   2.95

Andrew Ryder, S.C.J. In the East there is no sharp
distinction between prayer and theology. Far from being
divorced they are seen as supporting and completing
each other. One is impossible without the other.
Theology is not an end in itself, but rather a means, a
way to union with God.   ISBN: 0914544-47-0

THE RETURNING SUN
Hope for a Broken World   2.50

George A. Maloney, S.J. In this collection of meditations, the author draws on his own experiences rooted
in Eastern Christianity to aid the reader to enter into the
world of the "heart." It is hoped that through contemplation of this material he/she will discover the return of
the inextinguishable Sun of the universe, Jesus Christ,
in a new and more experiential way.   ISBN: 0-914544-42-X

FINDING PEACE IN PAIN
The Reflections of a Christian
Psychotherapist   3.50

Yvonne C. Hebert, M.A., M.F.C.C. For all who have ever
experienced the agony of loss of a loved one, loneli-
ness, handicap, abandonment, devastating illness. The
author draws the reader into the lives of those she has
counseled who have met such distressing life situa-
tions. She shares their experiences after following her
approach to overcoming their pain through prayer. Each
of the ten chapters clearly illustrates how this form of
prayer can transform life's hurts into opportunities for
emotional and spiritual growth.   ISBN: 0-914544-53-5

JOURNEY INTO CONTEMPLATION 3.95

George A. Maloney, S.J. This book is an in-depth handbook of guidance, inspiration and concrete advice. In it, Father Maloney provides sure teachings on deep union with God, discussing techniques, problems and anticipated rewards. Small groups who pray together contemplatively are also counseled. The author is a master retreat director and writer of many books, including our *The Returning Sun.* ISBN: 0-914544-51-9

ENCOUNTERING THE LORD IN DAILY
LIFE 3.95

Msgr. David E. Rosage. Delightfully spiced with humor and full of wisdom, this book is intended for all who would like to follow St. Paul's admonition to "pray constantly." Each of 52 chapters carry Scripture quotations which reinforce the weeks' message and focus new light on daily occurrences. This is a work helpful to all, particularly when we "don't have time to pray." Msgr. Rosage is the author of *Linger With Me* and other very popular Living Flame Press books. ISBN: 0-914544-45-4

PRAYING WITH MARY 2.95

Msgr. David E. Rosage. This book is one avenue which will help us discover ways and means to satisfy our longing for prayer and a more personal knowledge of God. Prayer was Mary's life-style. As we come to know more about her life of prayer we will find ourselves imitating her in our approach to God. ISBN: 0-914544-31-4

LINGER WITH ME
Moments Aside With Jesus 3.50

Rev. Msgr. David E. Rosage. God is calling us to a listening posture in prayer in the desire to experience Him at the very core of our being. Monsignor Rosage helps us to "come by ourselves apart" daily and listen to what Jesus is telling us in Scripture. ISBN: 0-914544-29-2

THE BOOK OF REVELATION:
What Does It Really Say? 2.50

John Randall, S.T.D. The most discussed book of the Bible today is examined by a Scripture expert in relation to much that has been published on the truth. A simply written and revealing presentation. The basis for many discussion groups. ISBN: 0-914544-16-0

WHOLENESS
The Legacy of Jesus   2.50

Adolfo Quezada presents practical and spiritual perspectives to those seeking purpose and meaning in their lives. He faces the reality that we are all broken by the impact of suffering and torn by the pull of distractions. He offers hope and direction toward a more abundant life.   ISBN: 0-914544-48-9

LIVING HERE AND HEREAFTER
Christian Dying,
Death and Resurrection   2.95

Msgr. David E. Rosage. The author offers great comfort to us by dispelling our fears and anxieties about our life after this earthly sojourn. Based on God's Word as presented in Sacred Scripture, these brief daily meditations help us understand more clearly and deeply the meaning of suffering and death.   ISBN: 0-914544-44-6

PRAYING WITH SCRIPTURE
IN THE HOLY LAND
Daily Meditations With the Risen Jesus   3.50

Msgr. David E. Rosage. Herein is offered a daily meeting with the Risen Jesus in those Holy Places which He sanctified by His human presence. Three hundred and sixty-five Scripture texts are selected and blended with the pilgrimage experiences of the author, a retreat master, and well-known writer on prayer.   ISBN: 0-914544-14-4

DISCERNMENT:
Seeking God in Every Situation   3.50

Rev. Chris Aridas. "Many Christians struggle with ways to seek, know and understand God's plan for their lives. This book is prayerful, refreshing and very practical for daily application. It is one to be read and used regularly, not just read" *(Ray Roh, O.S.B.).*   ISBN: 0-914544-37-3

A DESERT PLACE   2.50

Adolfo Quezada. "The author speaks of the desert place deep within, where one can share the joy of the Lord's presence, but also the pain of the nights of our own faithlessness" *(Pecos Benedictine).*   ISBN: 0-914544-40-3

MOURNING: THE HEALING JOURNEY   2.95

Rev. Kenneth J. Zanca. Comfort for those who have lost a loved one. Out of the grief suffered in the loss of both parents within two months, this young priest has written a sensitive, sympathetic yet humanly constructive book to help others who have lost loved ones. This is a book that might be given to the newly bereaved.

ISBN: 0-914544-30-6

THE BORN-AGAIN CATHOLIC   3.95

Albert H. Boudreau. This book presents an authoritative imprimatur treatment of today's most interesting religious issue. The author, a Catholic layman, looks at Church tradition past and present and shows that the born-again experience is not only valid, but actually is Catholic Christianity at its best. The exciting experience is not only investigated, but the reader is guided into revitalizing his or her own Christian experience. The informal style, colorful personal experiences, and helpful diagrams make this book enjoyable and profitable reading.

ISBN: 0-914544-26-8

WISDOM INSTRUCTS HER CHILDREN
The Power of the Spirit and the Word   3.50

John Randall, S.T.D. The author believes that now is God's time for "wisdom." Through the Holy Spirit, "power" has become much more accessible in the Church. Wisdom, however, lags behind and the result is imbalance and disarray. The Spirit is now seeking to pour forth a wisdom we never dreamed possible. This outpouring could lead us into a new age of Jesus Christ! This is a badly needed, most important book, not only for the Charismatic Renewal, but for the whole Church.

ISBN: 0-914544-36-5

DISCOVERING
PATHWAYS TO PRAYER   2.95

Msgr. David E. Rosage. Following Jesus was never meant to be dull, or worse, just duty-filled. Those who would aspire to a life of prayer and those who have already begun, will find this book amazingly thorough in its scripture-punctuated approach.

"A simple but profound book which explains the many ways and forms of prayer by which the person hungering for closer union with God may find him" *(Emmanuel Spillane, O.C.S.O., Abbot, Our Lady of the Holy Trinity Abbey, Huntsville, Utah).* ISBN: 0-914544-08-X

GRAINS OF WHEAT   2.95

Kelly B. Kelly. This little book of words received in prayer is filled with simple yet often profound leadings, exhortations and encouragement for daily living. Within the pages are insights to help one function as a Christian, day by day, minute by minute.   ISBN: 0-914544-32-2

BREAD FOR THE EATING   2.95

Kelly B. Kelly. Sequel to the popular *Grains of Wheat,* this small book of words received in prayer draws the reader closer to God through the imagery of wheat being processed into bread. The author shares her love of the natural world.   ISBN: 0-914544-39-X

DESERT SILENCE:
A Way of Prayer for an Unquiet Age   2.50

Alan J. Placa and *Brendan Riordan.* The pioneering efforts of the men and women of the early church who went out into the desert to find union with the Lord has relevance for those of us today who are seeking the pure uncluttered desert place within to have it filled with the loving silence of God's presence.

ISBN: 0-914544-15-2

WHO IS THIS GOD YOU PRAY TO?   2.95

Bernard Hayes, C.R. Who is God for me? How do I "picture" Him? This book helps us examine our negative images of God and, through prayer, be led to those images which Jesus reveals to us and which can help us grow into a deeper and more valid relationship with God as Father, Lover, Redeemer, etc.

ISBN: 0-914544-41-1

UNION WITH THE LORD IN PRAYER
Beyond Meditation to Affective
Prayer Aspiration and Contemplation   1.50

Venard Polusney, O.Carm. "A magnificent piece of work. It touches on all the essential points of contemplative prayer. Yet it brings such a sublime subject down to the level of comprehension of the 'man in the street,' and in such an encouraging way" *(Abbot James Fox, O.C.S.O., former superior of Thomas Merton at the Abbey of Gethsemane).*   ISBN: 0-914544-03-9

ATTAINING SPIRITUAL MATURITY
FOR CONTEMPLATION
(According to St. John of the Cross) 1.50

Venard Polusney, O. Carm. "I heartily recommend this work with great joy that at last the sublime teachings of St. John of the Cross have been brought down to the understanding of the ordinary Christian without at the same time watering them down. For all (particularly for charismatic Christians) hungry for greater contemplation" *(George A. Maloney, S.J., editor of Diakonia, Professor of Patristics and Spirituality, Fordham University).* ISBN: 0-914544-04-7

REASONS FOR REJOICING:
Experiences in Christian Hope 2.50

Rev. Kenneth J. Zanca. What is evil? Is all suffering evil? Why do I worship God? Is God really all powerful? With the expertise of an avid researcher and the guidance of a loving teacher, Fr. Zanca leads us to ponder the roots of our beliefs. He shows us that Christ has overcome the world, and that we do in reality have reasons to rejoice. Author also of, *The Judas Within* and *Mourning: The Healing Journey.* ISBN: 0-914544-12-8

THE TURNING ROAD:
One Man's Spiritual Journey 2.50

Ralph Kibildis. In case it can be thought that the flow of deep spiritual books is drying up, this work contradicts the idea . . . what he has written should prove extremely helpful to souls who are puzzled and struggling and in need of confidence. Dom Hubert van Zeller, O.S.B.
ISBN: 0-914544-34-9

TO COMFORT AND CONFRONT 2.95

Kenneth R. Overberg, S.J. God's Word challenges us and calls us again to conversion and growth. It invites us to ponder the experience of a God who takes delight in us, and to face the challenge of speaking the prophetic word in our own world. Individuals will find fresh insights for their private prayer. Communities and prayer groups will find stimulating starting points for shared prayer. The author teaches at Xavier University, Cincinnati. ISBN: 0-914544-49-7

PRESENCE THROUGH THE WORD   2.50

Sr. Evelyn Ann Schumacher, O.S.F. Divine revelation assures us that God's eternal plan in creating the universe is to give us not merely creative gifts but the gift of Himself. This simple but profound book shows that personal intimacy with the Father, the Son and the Holy Spirit is meant for every Christian. Sister also wrote *Pray With the Psalmist* and *Covenant Love.*

ISBN: 0-914544-46-2

PRAY WITH THE PSALMIST   2.50

Introduction by George A. Maloney, S.J.
Illustrated by Jacqueline Seitz
Sr. Evelyn Ann Schumacher, O.S.F. This is not a book about prayer but one which leads us into the experience of praying. This simple but profound book is a call to true conversion of heart, the indispensable starting point in anyone's life. The author blends her own prayerful experiences with those of the psalmist as together they move through the lights and darknesses common to all who truly seek God in prayer. Sister has also written *Covenant Love* and *Presence Through the Word.*

ISBN: 0-914544-33-0

COVENANT LOVE   2.50

Introduction by George A. Maloney, S.J.
Sr. Evelyn Ann Schumacher, O.S.F. In the form of dialog between God and the Christian, the author presents the gradual unfolding of the divine-human relationship as it is revealed in the Old Testament. The dialog then draws us into meditation on the New Covenant which was established by Jesus through His death and resurrection. This book powerfully provides some necessary background to a life of faith and prayer. Sister also wrote *Pray With the Psalmist* and *Presence Through the Word.*

ISBN: 0-914544-38-1

THE JUDAS WITHIN   2.50

Rev. Kenneth J. Zanca. Judas Iscariot, a much discussed figure, has often been seen in one dimension — completely evil and foreign to ourselves. But is he? Is there something within us that sometimes senses an affinity with him? Judas is here reexamined as he is portrayed in the Gospels. Through the author, we come to see the incredible mystery of God's love — a love so great it can embrace the darkness within Judas and ourselves. Father also wrote *Mourning: The Healing Journey* and *Reasons for Rejoicing.*   ISBN: 0-914544-25-X

LIVING FLAME PRESS

Box 74, Locust Valley, N.Y. 11560

QUANTITY

_____ Angel's Quest $6.95
_____ Attaining Spiritual Maturity 1.50
_____ Book of Revelation 2.50
_____ Born-Again Catholic 3.95
_____ Bread for the Eating 2.95
_____ Covenant Love 2.50
_____ Desert Place 2.50
_____ Desert Silence 2.50
_____ Discernment 3.50
_____ Discovering Pathways to Prayer 2.95
_____ Encountering the Lord in Daily Life 3.95
_____ Finding Peace in Pain 3.50
_____ Grains of Wheat 2.95
_____ Journey into Contemplation 3.95
_____ Judas Within 2.50
_____ Linger With Me 3.50
_____ Living Here and Hereafter 2.95
_____ Mourning 2.95
_____ Post Charismatic Experience 4.50
_____ Pray With the Psalmist 2.50
_____ Prayer: The Eastern Tradition 2.95
_____ Praying With Mary 2.95
_____ Praying With Scripture/Holy Land 3.50
_____ Presence Through the Word 2.50
_____ Reasons for Rejoicing 2.50
_____ Returning Sun 2.50
_____ Seeking Purity of Heart 2.50
_____ Spiritual Direction (Culligan) 5.95
_____ Thirsting for God in Scripture 2.95
_____ To Comfort and Confront 2.95
_____ Turning Road 2.50
_____ Union With the Lord 1.50
_____ Who Is This God You Pray To? 2.95
_____ Wholeness 2.50
_____ Wisdom Instructs Her Children 3.50

NAME _____

ADDRESS_____

CITY _____ STATE _____ ZIP _____

Payment enclosed. Kindly include $.70 postage and handling on orders up to $5; $1.00 on orders up to $10; more than $10 but less than $50 add 10% of total; over $50 add 8% of total. Canadian residents add 20% exchange rate, plus postage and handling.

52 - Wisdom is to discover God's plan &
move with it.

56 - Psalm 33 - The Lord brings to naught
the plans of the nations but the plan of
the Lord stands forever. (Get on God's
plan)

p. 51 Kings 3:9 Solomon prays - God,
give me wisdom so I can rule as you would
have me rule.

57 - Wisdom 7:22 - "Wisdom taught me (Solomon)
He is a Spirit intelligent, holy, unique &c.

59 1 Cor 1:30 God the Father made Christ
+ to be our wisdom & sanctification & justification -

LIVING FLAME PRESS
Box 74, Locust Valley, N.Y. 11560

QUANTITY

____ Angel's Quest $6.95
____ Attaining Spiritual Maturity 1.50
____ Book of Revelation 2.50
____ Born-Again Catholic 3.95
____ Bread for the Eating 2.95
____ Covenant Love 2.50
____ Desert Place 2.50
____ Desert Silence 2.50
____ Discernment 3.50
____ Discovering Pathways to Prayer 2.95
____ Encountering the Lord in Daily Life 3.95
____ Finding Peace in Pain 3.50
____ Grains of Wheat 2.95
____ Journey into Contemplation 3.95
____ Judas Within 2.50
____ Linger With Me 3.50
____ Living Here and Hereafter 2.95
____ Mourning 2.95
____ Post Charismatic Experience 4.50
____ Pray With the Psalmist 2.50
____ Prayer: The Eastern Tradition 2.95
____ Praying With Mary 2.95
____ Praying With Scripture/Holy Land 3.50
____ Presence Through the Word 2.50
____ Reasons for Rejoicing 2.50
____ Returning Sun 2.50
____ Seeking Purity of Heart 2.50
____ Spiritual Direction (Culligan) 5.95
____ Thirsting for God in Scripture 2.95
____ To Comfort and Confront 2.95
____ Turning Road 2.50
____ Union With the Lord 1.50
____ Who Is This God You Pray To? 2.95
____ Wholeness 2.50
____ Wisdom Instructs Her Children 3.50

NAME _____

ADDRESS_____

CITY _____ STATE _____ ZIP _____

Payment enclosed. Kindly include $.70 postage and handling on orders up to $5;
$1.00 on orders up to $10; more than $10 but less than $50 add 10% of total; over $50
add 8% of total. Canadian residents add 20% exchange rate, plus postage and han-
dling.

Copy - No one knows what lies at
the depth of God but the Spirit
of God. The Spirit we have
received is not the world's
Spirit but God's Spirit -
1 Cor 2:11-16

Copy - Sirach 4:11-19 Wisdom
instructs her children

Proph
Jeremiah 31:31 The days are
coming when I will make a new
covenant - -

Ezequiel 36:25 - - I will place
a new heart & a new Spirit within

p. 17 "Baptized in the Spirit" you
get into the ever-baptizing in the Spirit
says Steve Clark - there are stages &
stages - pride makes us think "we
have received it all" but - the beginning
of wisdom is to recognize how little you
really know"

p. 26 1 Cor 2:11 Eye has not seen ear yet
God has revealed this wisdom to us thru his Spirit

p. 46 - Isaiah 30:2 - no longer will your Teacher
Proph
hide from you - this is the way, walk in it

p. 48 Joel 3:1 I will pour out my Spirit...

p. 50 John 14:23 - we will come & make our home
in him - he will instruct you in everything